DENNIS HORN – RACING FOR AN ENGLISH ROSE

DENNIS HORN – RACING FOR AN ENGLISH ROSE

TRACK RACING IN THE 1930s

PETER UNDERWOOD

with contributions by Geoff Waters

Published in 2013

by:

Mousehold Press
Victoria Cottage
Constitution Opening
Norwich NR3 4BD

www.mousehold-press.co.uk

ISBN 978 1 874739 66 1

printed by Mimeo, Huntingdon

CONTENTS

1	Introduction	9
2	The Insularity of British Competitive Cycling: 1900 – 40	11
3	British Cycle Sport in the 1930s	16
4	The Cycling Life and Times of Dennis Horn	21
	Grass roots: Dennis' early racing days	
	1930: the breakthrough year	
	Hard-track times	
5	The Golden Years: 1932–1938	27
	A national track star	27
	1932	28
	1933	32
	1934	34
	1935	47
	1936	51
	1937	55
	1938	59
6	1939: A Year Too Far	64
7	Overview	68
Appendices		71
	A – The Job of Learning How	72
	B – Cultivating the Finishing Sprint	75
	C – Dennis Horn's Major Titles & Trophies: 1929–1938	77
	D – Dennis Horn's Track Racing Results: 1928–1939	79
References		81
About the authors		83

Acknowledgements:

We would like to express our heartfelt thanks to David Horn and Jackie Hopkinson (son and daughter of Dennis). We are greatly indebted to them for providing us with the the photographs of their father and other artefacts, as well as for all the help and encouragement they has given us in the preparation of this book.

We would also like to thank Mike Johnson of the Norwich Amateur Bicycle Club, Dennis Horn's club in the early 1930s, for providing us with valuable information and a list of programmes from that period.

Many thanks, too, to Colin Bedford, the restorer of Dennis Horn's Claud Butler 'DSH' track bike, for giving us with the opportunity to photograph it.

The English rose, worn on the rider's track vest.
Dennis won his first rose in 1930 when, at the age of 21,
he became the National Champion over 25 miles.

DENIS HORN

Cartoon of Dennis Horn, from the Programme of the
Good Friday meeting at Herne Hill, 1934

1

Introduction

My job of learning how began nearly seven years ago – when I was 15. My brother Cyril...brought Jack Sibbit to our home, and I was permitted to see the famous Manchester Wheeler's English rose, the emblem of a national championship.

...I determined there and then that one day I should wear an English rose upon my breast – like Jack...

A fortnight before my twenty–first birthday there was no prouder cyclist in England than I. My ambition, cherished for six long years, had come true; upon my vest was stitched a plain English rose – like Jack Sibbit's. I had won my first big race and it was the 25-mile (track) championship of England.

Dennis Horn, 'The Job of Learning How' (*Cycling* 10 July 1931)

During the 1930s, rural Fenland-born Dennis Horn, together with his older brother Cyril, rapidly graduated from the rough and tumble of makeshift grass track racing at country fairs to assailing the heights of British track cycling on the great urban cycling bastions of the time: the hard-surfaced banked outdoor stadiums of London's Herne Hill and Manchester's Fallowfield. In the process, both became national cycling stars, with Dennis overshadowing Cyril in terms of *palmarès*.

Dennis Sutton Horn was born on 5 July 1909 in the village of Upwell on the Norfolk/Cambridgeshire border; his father was a blacksmith who, at the time of Dennis's birth, operated five forges across the Fens, employing 14 men, mainly making horseshoes for the Army. But he was a man of diverse talents and interests: he was a bicycle maker, as were many blacksmiths at the turn of the century (and an early racing cyclist), a smallholder and for many years the licensee of the local pub. He was also a pioneer motorist who reportedly caused a stir in this tiny Fenland village when, in 1904, he turned up with a Daimler Waggonette, which became the official transport of the Upwell football team. Dennis's mother, Flossie Sutton came from a family whose local roots went back to the 17th century; they were known as a 'sporting' family.

Dennis had five siblings: two sisters and three brothers. His oldest brother Cyril, five years his senior, was an accomplished speed ice-skater who took to track cycling in the summer months as a means of keeping fit out of season. Dennis was to remain based in Upwell throughout his cycling career and settled in the area when he finally retired from competitive cycling at the end of 1939. He died in 1974 aged 65 and is buried in the village of Tilney All Saints near to his farm, which today remains in the family as a golfing and sports centre.

At first glance, the competitive cycling life story of Dennis Horn might appear to be a simple tale of a strapping rustic lad who, in time-honoured, heroic fashion, took on and beat the streetwise metropolitan champions of his era. Dennis certainly was an immensely powerful rider, capable of pushing gears as high as 96" on hard tracks to good effect, typically in extended high-speed sprint finishes to events of all distances. However, closer examination of his cycling career, together with that of his brother, suggests that in addition to becoming track stars in their own right, they were as astute as any of their urban contemporaries at treading the fine line between amateurism and professionalism as defined by the puritanical British cycling establishment of their day. Skills they probably learned from their father. That the flamboyant Claud Butler discreetly advertised an innovative eponymous 'DSH' (Dennis Sutton Horn) close clearance track model with upright angles in his celebrated range of lightweight machines is but one indication of this.

These two speedy yet savvy village lads rapidly established themselves as stars of the British summer track racing scene of the 1930s. It was a heady round of country fairs and gala sports days in provincial towns organised by the likes of local constabularies, along with fierce contests in major metropolitan centres for legendary gold and silver trophies at track meetings attended by thousands of spectators. However, this was a cycling scene entirely unique to Britain in the years before World War II.

In this racing biography of Dennis Horn, the nuances of cycle sport on track and road as practised primarily in Britain during the period 1900–1940 are explored first. The vicissitudes of Dennis' racing career both at home and abroad during the 1930s are then considered against the background of this distinctive era in the history of competitive cycling.

2

The Insularity of British Competitive Cycling:
1900–1940

In the first four decades of the 20th century competitive cycle sport as practised in the British Isles differed markedly from the way in which the sport was pursued in continental Europe in a number of key respects. The following table highlights the main differences.

Britain	Europe
Stringent amateurism was the norm with a strict set of rules limiting prizes, prize money, advertising and sponsorship. This amateur ideal was zealously policed and enforced at all levels of the sport by cycling's officialdom.	The status of 'amateur' was treated largely as a less lucrative stepping stone to a professional cycling career which was considered the acme of the sport.
Track racing was a summer sport pursued exclusively on outdoor grass and hard tracks.	With both outdoor and indoor velodromes, track racing on dedicated cement and wooden board tracks was a year-round activity with distinct summer and winter circuits.
The outdoor hard tracks were all large ovals with shallow bankings often encircling athletics tracks of some 440 yards in circumference.	Indoor tracks were short (less than 250 metres per lap) with steep bankings which also featured on even the largest outdoor velodromes.
Road racing was restricted to fixed distance individual time trials run discreetly over 'out and home' courses with competitors inconspicuously clad in alpaca jackets and black tights.	Mass start road racing was the norm with colourfully attired competitors forming highly visible pelotons on public roads in widely publicised one–day events and stage races.

Events on both road and track were based exclusively on the Imperial mile (1, 5, 10, 25, 50 and 100 miles) and fractions thereof (220, 440 and 880 yards).	The metric Kilometre was the basis of measurement in all branches of cycle sport.
The single fixed wheel system of gearing was *de rigueur* in all forms of cycle sport, with a front brake (as well as a bell) being mandatory for road time trials.	Mass start road racing pioneered the use of single freewheels with dual brakes and then the multi–speed 'derailleur' system of gearing.

In Britain and continental Europe different sets of status symbols in the form of distinctive awards, titles, trophies, jerseys and emblems were used to signify the prestige of cyclists whose racing achievements and performances were outstanding.

How was it that these two fundamentally different competitive cycling cultures – the one 'British', the other 'Continental' – came to exist as sporting traditions largely independently of and generally indifferent to one another? The answer lies squarely in the late 19th century, and in developments in the international relations between different national administrative cycling bodies in particular.

In the late 1800s competitive cycling, especially on dedicated cycling tracks, rapidly developed into a popular spectator sport in North America, the British Isles and mainland Europe. In the process, national cycling associations, like the League of American Wheelmen (est. 1880) and in Britain the National Cycling Union (est. 1883), were formed to govern the sport. In the early 1890s there was a move amongst these national governing bodies to create an international cycling authority to both legislate on cycling matters and hold annual official world championships.

This ultimately resulted in the formation of the International Cycling Association (ICA) in 1892, with its headquarters in London. Its foundation members were the cycling associations of the United Kingdom (which had pioneered the move), Belgium, Canada, Denmark, France, Germany, Holland, Italy and the United States. The Englishman Henry Sturmey (of Sturmey-Archer gear fame) was elected first president of the ICA. One of the ICA's earliest actions was to stage the first official world championships in 1893, in Chicago USA, to coincide with the 'World Fair' held in that city. It was resolved that these championships would be exclusively for amateurs.

However, even before the start, a conflict arose within the ICA between its various national representatives over the definition of 'amateur'. In this regard *Cycling,* published in 1972 by the Italian Olympic Committee, gives an Italian view of the circumstances surrounding the dispute:

Following the progressive development in Europe of the passion for the sport of bicycling, in 1892 the 'International Cyclist Association' [sic] was founded, with headquarters in London. This grouped together the national federations of America, Belgium, France, Canada, Germany, Holland, England and Italy; however, the presence of the Italian riders in the association was frowned on by the President of the ICA, Mr. Strurney [sic–*read Sturmey*], since the [Italian] UVI had allowed their riders to exchange the gold medals and silver cups won for their equivalent value in money.

One of the first acts of the ICA was to sponsor the world championships…at Chicago on the occasion of the great International Fair of 1893. The official bulletin of the ICA, published in London, expressed its determination to see the world championships limited to 'true amateurs' only and announced that it would offer a large gold–embroidered banner to the winner of the world speed championship over 1 mile.

But, when the banner arrived it was seen that the Italian crest was not included among those of the nations of the group of founder federations of the ICA. The affair became the object of a great deal of discussion. A number of affiliated federations protested, siding with Italy; but the English replied that they could not deflect from their principle of the purest amateurism and could not therefore place Italy…in contact with the other nations.'

(*Cycling, CONI*, 1972: 22–23)

It was thus the influential British representatives on the ICA whom the Italians blamed for the exclusion of Italian riders from the first ICA world championships. However, the amateur ideals of the ICA were subsequently repeatedly challenged by others during the 1890s. For instance, the American, A.A. Zimmermann, winner of the first ICA amateur sprint world championship, was sanctioned by the ICA for accepting 'exorbitant' prizes as well as sponsorship from Raleigh cycles. He responded by promptly turning professional and, presumably in an attempt to offset further such 'difficulties', the ICA relented and introduced professional world titles to complement the amateur ones in 1895. However, other cycling nations, most notably the French, continued to challenge the British hegemony in the ICA, as well as its adherence to the strictly amateur ideal. Matters finally came to a head at the turn of the century. The Italian version of these events is as follows:

> As a result of the non–participation of Italy in the first world championships and the offence rendered by the ICA to Italian cycling, the International Cycling Union (UCI) was born on the initiative first and foremost of the (Italian) UVI. The ICA within a few brief years remained an organisation without authority or following. Thus on March 14, 1900 the (UCI) was born, whose first congress took place on August 14, 1900 at Paris, and proved a triumph for Italian cycling, which had the satisfaction of seeing the headquarters of the newborn organisation fixed at Alessandria, with an Italian as its first President, in the person of Mr Mario Bruzzone.
> (*Cycling,* CONI, 1972: 23–24)

While it may be an exaggeration to suggest that it was solely the amateurism issue coupled with Italian discontent over it that ultimately destroyed the ICA, the fact remains that the defection of most leading cycling nations to the UCI not only shifted the centre of international administrative power in the sport to mainland Europe, but left British cycling internationally isolated. The NCU was to belatedly affiliate to the UCI in 1903. By then, however, the die was already cast. Britain was now reduced to having only marginal influence in world cycling affairs, which meant that the ideal of stringent amateurism could only be enforced and perpetuated in British cycle sport, which is precisely what occurred. However, this was not unusual in Britain at that time since most other sporting codes there remained strictly amateur, with the 'Corinthian' spirit having been a cornerstone of national sporting culture since early Victorian times. In this regard, contemporary foreign observers are reported as wryly quoting the former British Prime Minister, Lord Rosebery's observation in 1900 to the effect that, 'It is beginning to be hinted that we are a nation of amateurs'.

But it was not only international relations which had so crucial an impact on the shape and culture of cycle sport in Britain during the period before

World War II. In the 1890s road racing in Britain itself faced a crisis. Under the heading, 'The British way', the incomparable 20th century cycling journalist, J. B. Wadley, succinctly summarises these domestic developments:

> When, at the turn of the century, "mass start" racing was finally abandoned following continual harassment by the police, British road sport followed a trail of its own which was destined to keep it apart from the mainstream of European competition for more than 40 years. Some ... give thanks that the severance resulted in the development of an entirely different form of road sport which gave British cycling a character of its own. On the continent of Europe the time trial is a rare item on the racing programme. In Britain the time trial is a way of life. (Wadley, 1975: 73)

This, then, was the distinctively British competitive cycling world which Dennis Horn and his contemporaries bestrode in the period immediately before World War II. However, to fully appreciate Dennis' racing achievements a clear examination of the main forms of cycle sport in which he participated is warranted.

3

British Cycle Sport in the 1930s

During the 1930s the bulk of cycle sport in the UK consisted of clandestine time trials held at the crack of dawn, ridden by amateur riders dressed from top to toe in black, including the ubiquitous alpaca jacket. The events were regulated first by the Road Racing Council (RRC) and from 1938 by the Road Time Trial Council (RTTC). In an attempt to appease the police's resistance to cycle racing on the road it was felt that this formula would keep the sport low-key enough to avoid public hostility. The venues were closely guarded and known only by secret codes. These time trials were run at distances of 25, 50 and 100 miles, plus timed events of 12 and 24 hours.

The shorter distance events would be over and everyone dispersed by about 8am in the summer months, but the longer events would carry on surreptitiously through the day, with up to a hundred entrants plus marshals and feeding stations skulking around the courses.

The powers that be, in the form of the NCU and RTTC, did all they could to discourage any thoughts of massed-start road racing. This remained the case until Percy Stallard formed the British League of Racing Cyclists (BLRC) in 1942, which staged the revolution.

As a complete contrast to this state of affairs, well-publicised track racing was held at many venues around the country ranging from small village fêtes to large-scale international events at purpose-built cycle tracks. These events could draw crowds of tens of thousands. Grass-track events were often run by commercial companies, such as Cadbury's. Some of the events were designated national, district or area championships and had the extra kudos of the title to be won as well as the prize list.

At some of the track meetings held on both grass and hard tracks the prizes consisted of a silver, or in some rare cases, even a gold cup. The Muratti Vase, for example, was solid gold and was sponsored by a well-known cigarette manufacturer, and another was the Vi-Tonica Gold Cup. Dunlop and other cycle-related companies also presented valuable trophies. A successful track rider could win one of these outright should he be the victor three times. Top sprinters even turned down offers to compete in the Olympic Games or World Championships when they were in a position of holding two 'stakes' in such a trophy. It has to be remembered that in those days travel overseas would be by boat and the total time away from the UK could add up to several weeks for events like the Olympics when they were held in America in 1932. This wiped out a fair part of a home season, as well as resulting in the loss of a lot of working time.

TEA INTERVAL.

FIRST RACE AFTER TEA AT 5·30 SHARP.

Event 15.—5·30. One Mile Open Bicycle Handicap

First Prize, 4-Piece Pewter Tea Set and 4 Royal Doulton Cups and Saucers on double folding Tea Stand, value £5

Second „ Luncheon Set on Tray, value £2/10/-

Third „ Chromium Plated Clock, value £1/5/-

First in each Heat and two fastest Seconds to compete in Final

First Heat.

No.	Competitor's Name	Name of Club	yards
9	Cole, C.	Luton Wheelers	84
27	Hatten, G.	Cambs. T and CCC	130
11	Gatward, K. A.	Cambs. T and CCC	165
14	Griffin, E. W.	Morton Wheelers	170
24	Woollard, J. F.	Unattatched	175
30	Howard, W. D.	Cambs. T and CCC	180
3	Light, W. E.	Cambs. T and CCC	190

First   Second   Time

Second Heat.

8	Horn, D. S.	Norwich ABC	Scr.
26	Howlett, A.	Cambs. T and CCC	120
2	Balaam, A. F.	Cambs T and CCC	145
6	Byatt, J. E.	Bishop Stortford A and CC	170
25	Woollard, A. G.	Unattached	175
21	Bedford, C. W.	Huntingdon Wheelers	180
1	Johnson. F. A.	Cambs. T and CCC	190

First   Second   Time

Third Heat.

12	Carter, L. B.	Cambs. T and CCC	90
85	Lewis, A. H.	Cambs. T and CCC	130
10	Cox, R.	Lincoln Wellington	138
29	Smith, G.	Norwich ABC	170
16	Judd, P. K.	Huntingdon Wheelers	170
17	Wright, J. W.	Bishops Stortford A and CC	185
23	Woollard, P. J.	Cambs. T and CCC	195

First   Second   Time

14

From the Programme of the Waterbeach & District Horticultural Society's Annual Sports Day, held on August Bank Holiday Monday, 1933. Dennis is riding off scratch in the one-mile handicap. Note the typical prize list.

There was a distinct pecking order amongst the top echelon of riders, who would be 'pot-hunting' over the season, travelling from event to event getting their name on a chosen trophy and hoping eventually to win it outright. As in most sports, there was a large supporting cast competing for the minor places, but always with the hope of taking a top scalp on the right day. To make things more interesting, many events were held on a handicap basis with the fastest ('scratch') rider sometimes starting up to half a lap behind the first man off in a four lap event.

Village sports were run by local committees and might well incorporate athletics and other novelty events. The rules of amateurism were very strict and the merest hint of a cash prize could result in a minimum of one year's suspension. Nevertheless, riders with improbable (and almost certainly fictitious) names raced for cash in the Scottish Highland Games.

To obtain prizes the organisers trawled around local shops with a begging bowl. Some retailers would generously donate a reasonable prize. On the other hand, some became fed up with this endless begging by every local society and scoured the shop looking for some dusty old unsold item. The results of this could often lead to the prize presentation looking like a 'White Elephant' stall.

In the early years of the decade the lucky few might win the prize of a joint of meat or string of sausages from the local butchers. This could be the ration for a family of four for a week in the prewar years, as some people rarely had meat unless it was caught in the wild. At local grass-tracks held in rural areas a farmer might donate a bag of potatoes or a runt from the litter of pigs that would surely die if left to fend for itself. However, this could create problems as most competitors cycled to events on their track machines, with sprint wheels mounted on wheel carriers for the journey out and back. Dick Hampton, a V-CC member, tells the following tale:

> My father used to be a successful grass-track racer, he was a farmer
> with a smallholding and used to keep pigs. He topped up his stock
> by winning them at village sports/cycle meetings. At many meetings
> the first prize in the main race was a young pig given by a local
> farmer. The farmer would of course pick the smallest of the litter,
> namely the runt. At the end of the meet we would head for home
> on the track bikes (with a single brake fitted for the journey). In
> those days there were only brown paper carrier bags, no plastic of
> course, and the pig would be stood in one of these hanging by the

handles over the handlebars. Its two front feet and head would be poking over the top of the bag. All was well for the first part of the journey until the pig got overexcited, probably speeding down a hill with father pedalling like mad on the fixed-wheel. The excitement would be too much for the pig's bladder control and in no time the bottom of the bag was soaked and the first of the hind legs would shoot through the bottom. The race was then on to get home before the bottom gave way completely and the pig would land on the road and head off as fast as its (soaked) legs would carry it, chased by the family, who would have to take turns carrying the pig home under one arm whilst riding on fixed. When we got home the pig would be carefully fed by hand until it was big enough to fend for itself.

Should these local events make a profit, the bonus might be put towards financing the next year's event or was often donated to charity.

The bikes used for grass-track racing changed through the 1930s. The early frames had quite slack angles and long fork rakes, long top tubes and short stems. As some of the riders visited the Continent and continental riders competed in the UK, towards the second half of the decade angles became more upright, fork rake and clearances reduced, and with shorter top tubes the stems became longer. Most people were riding tubulars on the track, wood sprint rims were quite popular on grass and often the tyres, especially the front, were taped on for extra security. More serious riders favoured the inch-pitch block and chains, believed to give an instant response to a kick on the pedals. These were also stronger as there were fewer moving parts. Although Chater-Lea chainsets were very popular, track riders often used the BSA 5-pin chainset as it was judged to have stronger cranks. One setback with the BSA was the need to remove pedals to change the rings. With inch-pitch it was often necessary to juggle with the rings and sprockets to get the desired gearing as there were only half the options compared with a half-inch set-up.

At the end of the decade, with the outbreak of WWII, development of the sport stopped. Small scale cycling events took place, but energies were focussed on the war effort by those left at home. Many of those who had been involved in cycle sport were called up for military service and had very little time for recreation, even if they were stationed in the UK rather than overseas. It was the end of an era.

4

The Cycling Life and Times of Dennis Horn

Given the split personality of interwar British amateur competitive cycling, the choice which faced the ambitious sporting cyclist of that era was a stark one: either embrace the introverted, cult like world of road time trials or opt for the extrovert, colourful and publicity orientated NCU track racing scene. It was perhaps inevitable that a country lad as cheerful and bluff as Dennis Horn reputedly was, would be drawn to the latter and, apart from indulging in the occasional early season local 25-mile time trial, would remain a dedicated 'trackie' for his entire cycling career.

In making this choice Dennis was undoubtedly heavily influenced by his older brother Cyril. Cyril had started his sporting career as a speed ice-skater in the Fens, going on to win National Championships and to represent the UK in the 1924 Winter Olympics. In common with other skaters in Europe, Cyril later took up cycling to keep himself fit in the summer months, as both sports use similar muscles. In May 1927 he joined Cambridge (Town & County) CC. It was Cyril who first brought Jack Sibbit to their village home where Jack's trademark sleeveless vest with its British championship rose emblem so impressed the teenage Dennis, inspiring him with the ambition of ultimately winning a rose motif for himself.

Jack Sibbit (1895–1950), while one of the most influential and colourful figures in 20th century British cycle sport, has been largely forgotten in the UK, but he raced at the highest level until well into his 40s, won many national track titles and major track events, and represented Britain with distinction at both the Olympics and UCI world championships. He later became a cycling official and team manager, mentor and coach to the young Reg Harris and produced hand-built track machines of the best quality. Sibbit was to be one of Dennis' main rivals during the 1930s, although they also raced successfully together as tandem partners, with Jack as captain and Dennis as stoker.

Grass roots: Dennis' early racing days

It is not clear as to when exactly it was that Dennis first turned a crank in anger. What is known, however, is that in April 1928 he joined the Cambridge (Town and Country) Cycling Club, following in the wheel tracks of his brothers Cyril and Reg, both of whom had become Cambridge T&CCC members the previous summer. Possibly their choice of club was influenced by the Cambridge club having a more active presence in the track racing scene than their local club, Wisbech Wheelers. Certainly it was at Cyril's instigation that the Cambridge club came to organise regular evening grass-track meetings with prize money of £1 10s, £1 and 10 shillings for the first three places in their events – an innovation which apparently came close to bankrupting the club. By the autumn of 1927 Cyril had become captain of the Cambridge track team.

Nationally he quickly became as competitive in the world of cycle sprinting as he was at skating. He was to win a National Championship, the 25-mile Sprint* in 1931, the 1-mile Grass Championship in 1933 and the 1,000-yard Sprint in 1937. He was also included in the British squad for many international events. Dennis, younger by five years, was already following the path of both disciplines, but whereas Cyril was the stronger skater, Dennis was the more successful of the two on the track once he had learned the craft. Having said that, Cyril was no slouch and was in the top handful of sprinters in the country, it was just that Dennis nearly always had the edge on him when they raced against each other.

Dennis' name first began to feature in the results of grass-track meetings in his native eastern counties during the summer of 1928, when he was 19 years of age. Over the season he won one race (the 1-mile handicap at the Norwich ABC meeting in late August) and finished third on five other occasions. Clearly he made rapid progress in his first year in the colours of the Cambridge club.

It was in the summer track season of 1929 that Dennis first really began to make his mark on the local grass-track scene. Over the course of that year he was in the first three in a total of 33 grass-track events, winning eight races, finishing second in 19 and third in six. His most notable victory came in May when he won the 10-mile NCU Eastern Counties

---

* It is worth noting in this regard that in Britain at that time the term 'sprint' was used as a generic term for all types of track events as distinct from the 'match sprint' event which was essentially a distinctly European/UCI invention.

Centre Championship held at the Norwich Charity Sports meeting. He thus became a rider for his provincial rivals to watch out for. More often than not, however, Dennis was still playing second fiddle to brother Cyril, who proved to be a prolific winner. Together the brothers became a formidable team, no doubt inspiring talk of the 'Horn mafia' amongst their fellow competitors.

Their formidable performances in local events is best illustrated over the August Bank holiday weekend where they competed in four separate events. Upwell Sports would have been literally on their doorstep as they were living in the village. In three events, the Half-mile, 3-mile and the 2-mile point-to-point Cyril was first and Dennis second.

Next it was to the Suffolk coast for the Benacre Sports. Benacre was hosting the Quarter-mile NCU (Eastern Counties Centre) Championship, which Cyril won with Dennis second. The places were the same for the Half-mile Scratch, but Dennis won the 1-mile race. Although this would have entailed a long drive, no doubt they felt it was worth it to compete in, and win, the Centre Championship.

The third event of the weekend was just outside Cambridge at the home of Chivers jam, Histon, where the big event of the day was the 6-lap County Scratch – Cyril first and Dennis second. In the 3-lap event, their club-mate, L. B. Carter, was the winner, with Dennis second and Cyril third. Cyril won the 3-lap Scratch ahead of F. H. Wyld of Derby RC, then one of the top sprinters in the country. Dennis won the 4-lap race. Yet another event was squeezed in over this weekend, possibly on the Tuesday evening.

Close to Peterborough is Whittlesey, famous for the production of bricks. The skyline was dominated by vast chimneys from the kilns, where thousands of workers would have been employed. Here was held the British Legion Sports, where Dennis came second in the Half-mile. In the one-lap Quarter-mile Scratch Cyril won with Dennis second, but Dennis came back to take the Mile-and-a-half race. The big event of the day would have been the Eastern Counties NCU Half-mile Championship, which was again a Horn 1-2 with Cyril first and Dennis second. In the final 1-Mile race Dennis was second.

In early September 1929 the two brothers appeared at a major British hard-track meeting for the first time. The occasion was the NCU National 5-mile Championship held at London's historic Herne Hill stadium. While neither reached the final of the event, it nevertheless represented a significant step forward in both of their racing careers. This was their first experience as smaller fishes in a big pond, rather than the big fishes in the relatively small local pond. Better was to come.

1930: the breakthrough year

This was the year in which Dennis turned 21 and it marked his emergence from the comparative backwaters of the sport into the national arena. For him the highlight of the year was winning the 25-mile NCU National Championship on the Derby track on 30 June in front of a crowd of 8,000. He thereby realised his teenage dream inspired by Jack Sibbit, and was entitled to wear the coveted English rose emblem on his track vest. According to press reports of the race, the two Horn brothers controlled matters throughout, aggressively riding at the front of the main field of 20 men and chasing down all attempted breakaways until the final sprint for the line, when Dennis launched himself to victory. While perhaps a curiosity to modern cyclists, in the interwar years the 25-mile British national track title had immense cachet in the UK and catapulted Dennis into the national limelight for the first time.

Once there, he did not disappoint, and a few weeks later finished a close second to Jack Sibbit in the 10-mile contest at Manchester's Fallowfield stadium for the legendary gold Muratti Cup. In August, *Cycling* magazine was prompted to ask whether Dennis was 'A future sprint champion?'

Overall, Dennis' racing results for the summer season of 1930 differed markedly from those of previous summers. He now figured in hard-track results, winning three races (including the national 25) and finishing second three times. On grass tracks his results were four firsts, four seconds and two wins. He was well on his way to national stardom.

An end-of-season report in *Cycling* at the end of November entitled 'The Year's Path Sport' noted:

> Consistent success upon grass has been scored by the Horn brothers (Cambridge TCCC) and on one afternoon at Norwich, Dennis Horn won the King's Cup, secured third place in the lap handicap, won the three-mile Scratch race and was unfortunate to puncture while defending his title as the Eastern Counties 10-mile Champion.

The item went on:

> Later came the 25-mile championship which brought together the majority of the crack riders of the country; it was surprisingly,

though meritoriously, won by D S Horn who, owing to the situation of his home must necessarily race mainly upon grass tracks, but is strikingly fast at such times as he does appear upon a cement surface. His success on this occasion was no surprise to those who had followed his career at the country meetings during the earlier part of the season.

Reading through the various reports in *Cycling* throughout the year, one could detect a slightly condescending attitude towards the Horns, sometimes referring to them as 'provincial riders' and being less than complimentary about their riding style, particularly that of Dennis. This was a time when London was smarting at the fact that they were producing no real winners on the track to counter the Manchester and other North Country winners. It probably irked them that Dennis and Cyril had appeared from the Fens, where there was no hard track to race on, and had started to win races, including championships, all over the place. To rub salt into the wounds Dennis had, of course, notched his first National Championship by beating some of the best riders in the whole country. *Cycling* had, however, on 1 August, in its series, 'Biographies of Racing Men, featured D. S. Horn as 'a Fenlander with a future'!

Hard-track times
In 1930, while Dennis Horn was busy making a name for himself in the carnival atmosphere of British track racing, the gentleman-journalists of *Cycling* magazine established the season long 'British Best All Rounder' (BBAR) competition for their much-cherished world of road time trialing. *Cycling*'s generally restrained coverage of British track racing at this time implies an editorial view of it as being a little too flashy, attracting flamboyant 'trade' characters like the lightweight manufacturer, Claud Butler. Road time trialing and the BBAR in particular were what really mattered. However, as one leading modern cycling writer observes:

> Time trialing existed in a vacuum, cut off from international cycling, so for years many of the best British cyclists ended up racing their hearts out for purely national honours; the only world championship discipline that bore any resemblance to it was the individual pursuit. (Fotheringham, 2010: 380)

Track racing was thus effectively the only branch of the sport in the 1930s in which British cyclists could hope to measure themselves against international opposition. In the years to come Dennis Horn was to earn numerous opportunities to do so, and during his career he was to have more international racing experience, both at home and abroad, than any of his British time trialing contemporaries could ever dream of.

In August 1931 Dennis was selected (along with Sibbit, Cozens and Higgins) to represent Britain at the UCI World Track Championships in Copenhagen, Denmark. All were to compete in the amateur 1,000-metres match sprint – an event which the NCU had only recently seen fit to introduce as an official British national championship to replace the ¼ mile, 1-mile and 5-mile titles. This brought British track cycling more into line with international UCI practice. But the tardiness of the NCU in doing so is made all the more remarkable by past British achievements: Bill Bailey won the UCI World Amateur Sprint title four times before the First World War and 'Tiny' Johnson won it in 1922. This was Dennis' first sortie abroad in national colours. However, while gaining experience in this specialised event, none of the British riders could match the skilled Continental sprinters in this discipline on their steeply banked track, and all failed to qualify for the last eight. The 1931 amateur world title was eventually won by the Dane, Helge Harder, with his fellow countryman Falk Hansen taking the pro title from the reigning champion, Frenchman Lucien Michard. This latter result was allegedly due to a judging error in the final which the UCI refused to reverse since the result had already been officially announced.

But if Dennis failed to make an impression at the 1931 World Championships, he went from strength to strength on the shallow banked hard tracks at home. Specialising in what would today be considered 'endurance' track events, he won the Rudge–Whitworth Cup at Herne Hill and then the Dunlop Cup at Coventry. However, his greatest success of 1931 was his winning of the 10-mile event for the fabled Muratti Cup at Fallowfield before a crowd of 18,000, beating home favourite, Jack Sibbit, into third place. Although Percy Wyld took several of the intermediate lap prizes, Jack Sibbit had his eye on Dennis, whom he considered to be the biggest danger, and kept glued to his wheel. On the final lap Ernie Chambers led into the back straight but Dennis, who was two lengths behind, shot by with a powerful sprint to win by a length. Chambers finished second and Jack Sibbit, who could not match Dennis's sprint, finished third.

Manchester had always been regarded as the home of track racing, somewhat to the chagrin of the Herne Hill organisers who had been debating over the previous winter how to make track racing more popular. It seems obvious that the success of the Manchester Wheelers' riders had generated great support for the sport in their area whereas London was just not able to produce top-rank track sprinters.

By the end of the season Dennis had scored a total of 12 wins, six on grass and six on hard tracks, and in a poll amongst the readers of *Cycling* he was voted joint 'Best Pathman of the Year', along with the then 36-year-old Jack Sibbit. Perhaps even more significantly, Dennis was also awarded the Meredith Memorial Trophy for accruing the highest number of points from selected prestige track events over the season. This trophy honoured Leon Meredith (1883–1930), who had been the UCI amateur world paced track champion seven times before the First World War and was subsequently the owner of the 'Constrictor' tyre and component company.

At age 22 Dennis had clearly matured into a track rider of considerable stature and in the winter of 1931/32 he left the Cambridge T&CCC for the presumably greener pastures of the Norwich Amateur Bicycle Club.

5

The Golden Years: 1932-38

A national track star

By the start of the summer track season of 1932 Dennis had established himself as a nationally recognised track rider on both grass and hard tracks, and was rapidly becoming one of the stars of British track racing. As a result he was much sought after by track meeting promoters and organisers nationwide and was in a position to pick and choose his events and plan his summer racing programme accordingly.

Each year he targeted high profile track meetings and events on both grass and hard tracks. These included specific valuable trophies like the Muratti Cup, which could potentially be won outright, as well as national and regional track titles at various distances. A regular season's goal was to win the Meredith Memorial Trophy.

Typically the brothers' racing season began slowly – Dennis regularly admitting that he only started serious training in February, and that he would first test himself in a local early season 25-mile road time trial. His first track meeting of the year would be the Herne Hill Good Friday meeting, but he was rarely at his best there. As the summer progressed Dennis and Cyril were regulars at Herne Hill, Fallowfield, Derby and Coventry hard-track meetings. Interspersed with these were grass-track meetings at venues widely scattered throughout the country – Portsmouth, Birmingham, Pontypool, Bristol, Exmouth, Ely and Glasgow – both for weekend and midweek events. So, during successive summers, Dennis and Cyril lived a traveller's life and journeyed extensively together by car to reach race meetings. Their motto could well have been: 'Have track bike, will travel'. What made the brothers' endeavours all the more remarkable is that this was accomplished in a period when car ownership in Britain was low, the road network rudimentary and it was an era of national austerity.

Moreover, if they were to avoid risking being 'sent to Coventry' by the NCU they had to maintain the appearance of being strictly amateur. That they were able to follow such a peripatetic racing lifestyle every summer throughout the 1930s without financial support and inducements is, in retrospect, frankly unbelievable. Officially, the NCU would only authorise race organisers to reimburse riders for their train fares – at third-class rate. At the very least, what this suggests is that the NCU hierarchy were complicit in the 'financial arrangements' made by top trackmen, provided these remained discreet. They must have realised that it was these unacknowledged arrangements which made the NCU's rich annual summer programme of track events a success. The funding in both cash and kind enabled the stars to travel to participate in race meetings throughout the country and, in so doing, attracted the paying public in large numbers. And sometimes the numbers were enormous. For instance, in 1932 a grass track in Wales reportedly had 30,000 spectators; Manchester's Fallowfield regularly had crowds of between 15,000 and 20,000; and at London's Herne Hill concerns were raised when gate attendances at track meetings fell below 8,000 people.

In common with most of their contemporaries, Dennis and Cyril rode races of all distances and types, ranging from the one-lap dash through to the 25-mile. Their races included both handicaps, in which riders start at staggered intervals around the track, and scratch races as well as 'match sprints'. Dennis was also an accomplished track tandemist, both as stoker and occasionally as captain.

Over the course of his racing caree, Dennis established himself as a leading member of the elite inner circle of versatile track racing stars in the Britain of the 1930s. His was one of the 'names' which drew the crowds to the celebrated outdoor meetings on both grass and hard tracks in the summers of the last decade before the war.

1932

Over the winter the NCU governing body decided to instigate grass-track championships for the next season onwards at one and five-miles. This move was resisted by Manchester Wheelers who, having a hard track, felt that championships should be confined to these surfaces. There was, however, a feeling in the rest of the country that the vast numbers of cyclists who only had the chance to race on grass tracks at local cycling/athletics meetings should be recognised. As an illustration of its popularity, in July 30,000 people watched the grass-track racing at Pontypool, a gate which would certainly have been looked upon enviously at Fallowfield or Herne Hill.

At Herne Hill over the Easter weekend Dennis was in surprisingly good form for this early period of the year. Now riding under the colours of Norwich Amateur Bicycle Club, he won the 550-yards Scratch Race from Ernie Chambers and Jack Sibbit on Good Friday, and the Invitation 70-lap Madison Race on Easter Monday. Unusually, he was partnered in the Madison not by Cyril but by F. V. Barnes of Marlborough CC; they beat the Wyld brothers into second place, with Cyril, paired with F. W. Southall of the Norwood Paragon, third.

Cycling's report on this meeting predicted that Jack Sibbit and Dennis would be pairing up for the forthcoming National Tandem Championships and would be going to Herne Hill to train a week before the race. Interviewed about this Dennis said he had no real interest in tandem racing except for championships or the Olympics, but that he would not be going to the Olympics. Six weeks in the United States would entail six weeks away from the UK scene with its many lucrative events and trophies to be won.

In spite of this, a half-page advert appeared in *Cycling* in April 1932 heralding the Olympic Cycling Trials to be held at Herne Hill at the end of the month which mentioned Dennis in two of the highlighted paragraphs. One stated: 'In the sprint is Higgins improving on his 1931 form? Will Dennis Horn beat him? Is Harry Wyld to be considered?' The other raised the questions: 'Are the Chambers Brothers a better tandem pair than the previous Chambers-Sibbit combination? Will Sibbit and Dennis Horn nick?'

In the tandem races at the Olympic Trials Dennis did ride behind Jack Sibbit and they did win, in spite of Sibbit 'loitering' to gain position and nearly losing out. Tandems need much more effort to wind up and Jack left them barely enough time to do this. As a consequence of their win, the NCU decided to allow Dennis a week in which to re-consider whether he could make the trip to Los Angeles. His mind was made up, however. There were cups to be won back home.

In May the Horns were at Coventry for the Rover Racing Club Sports, where Dennis 'brought off a useful double against first-class rivals' as *Cycling* put it. He won the Jordison Bowl in the half-mile Scratch Race and the Dunlop Cup for the 5-mile Scratch. In June they were back in the Midlands for the Annual Midland C & AC/Bourneville AC event. This was to be the first holding of the newly promoted One-mile National Grass Championship and Dennis won it convincingly.

Two days later he was back with Jack Sibbit for the One-mile NCU National Tandem Championship at Herne Hill, and again they came out on top. Powering round the others, and dictating the tactics, they were able to win easily. After convincing wins at both the Olympic Selections and the National Championships, Claud Butler was able to claim absolute superiority at both tandem events in his advertising. At that time tandems were an important part of his business.

The excellent form that Sibbert and Dennis showed when they were together on a tandem did not prevent their intense rivalry on solos. In the 25-mile National Championships on the Derby Municipal track, which Cyril had won the year before, Dennis controlled the race for the whole distance, winding in anyone trying to make a break and eventually winning by a length and a half from Jack Sibbit.

Then, back at Herne Hill, Jack Sibbit retained the Sprint Championship of England. He had been hotly tipped to win this 1,000-yards title, and went into the deciding race against Dennis and Ernie Chambers. Dennis was adjudged to have run Sibbit wide on the last corner and was disqualified from his second place. Dennis had been in the lead and was watching for his two opponents, first he looked to his left and in so doing swerved to the right, forcing Sibbit wide and up the banking. Sibbit took matters into his own hands, literally, by grabbing Dennis's seat pin and holding him back whilst he sprinted. If the judges had considered the race as a whole they might well have ordered a re-run, but they took the easy way out and disqualified Dennis and awarded the title to Jack.

Somehow during that same weekend the Horn brothers also raced at Manchester City Police Sports, where Dennis won the quarter-mile Scratch Race and came third in the 5-mile Scratch Race. A sign of the times, perhaps, on this same weekend there were events organised by no fewer than six constabularies – a good time for the burglars to get some work done!

The Norwich ABC Sports on 3 July was something of a Horn benefit: Dennis was first and Cyril second in the 1,000-yards Championship and in the one-lap Scratch race, and Cyril was first with Dennis second in the race for the club's 5-mile Championship.

The following weekend *Cycling* reported Dennis as 'the Governor' after his victories in both the 10-mile and the sprint at the Manchester Wheelers' Meet:

Scratch racing at the Manchester Wheelers' Meet last Saturday proved once again that D. S. Horn is the complete governor of the track-racing world this season. Although it is Sibbit's home track, the Fenlander won both the sprint race for the Vi-tonica Cup and the 10-mile for the Muratti Cup. Sibbit was second in both races in front of a crowd of 17,000.

A few days later the British team left for the Olympics on the Empress of Britain, with many commentators bemoaning the fact neither Dennis nor Jack Sibbit were on board, and querying whether it was worth sending a team of our second-best riders.

While the British team was in America, Dennis set the seal on his superiority on grass when he won the first 5-Mile National Grass-track Championship which was held at Batley in the face of keen competition, not only from the local riders, but also from other leading track stars of the country. From the start it was going to be a go-all-the-way affair. Dennis covered the leaders and went through in second place on most laps. At the bell, with only six of the fifteen entrants having survived the blistering pace, Dennis moved to the front and wasn't challenged as he went on to win by eight lengths.

At the end-of-season NCU Meeting at Herne Hill Dennis won the 440-yards Invitation Scratch Race and with it the Meredith Memorial Track Trophy. In its race report on the Herne Hill meeting, *Cycling* commented: 'The conditions seemed to suit the "push, shove and stamp on them" methods of D. S. Horn.'

They were back at Herne Hill again the following weekend, before a crowd of 5,000, for the Meeting of Champions. The organisers had signed up two Germans – Toni Merkens and the new World Champion, Teddy Richter – to compete against Dennis Horn and Jack Sibbit in an International Match Race series which the Germans won. Although some of the finishes were as close as six inches, it must be said they won easily.

The points gained from this meet gave Dennis an even more convincing win in the Meredith Memorial Track Trophy, with 52 points against the second place Sibbit who had 23 – Cyril was fifth with 12 points.

Looking forward to the 1933 season, *Cycling* commented:

Taking the existing sprinters, it is quite obvious that on last year's racing D. S. Horn would be a certainty for the Sprint Championship at Fallowfield, failing any foreign cracks competing. If Horn is to be beaten there then only the locals can do it. Sibbit, who won the title in 1931 at Fallowfield and did it again in London last year, is approaching veterancy, but as keen as ever and preparing for another season, but Horn clearly had the beating of him for the whole of the second half of the season.

1933

In July Manchester Wheelers organised its major event at the Fallowfield stadium. Dennis won the Invitation Sprint for the Vi-tonica Cup, with Sibbit second and Ernest Higgins third. In the race for the Muratti Gold Cup Dennis came out on top again, thereby winning this gold cup outright. He had acquired the habit of pinpointing the events with valuable trophies that could be won in this way. Jack Sibbit was again second and the Frenchman, Charles Rampelberg, third, and a crowd of 12,000 showed the keenness of the Manchester cyclists for track racing.

The following Monday evening a 'revenge' match was organised at Herne Hill. Rampelberg won the Sprint final from Dennis, but the Horn brothers won the 50-lap Madison with the Dusika and Rampelberg team beaten into second place. Cyril and Dennis would have driven from Manchester to their home in Upwell on the Saturday evening and then driven from Upwell to Herne Hill, in south London, on the Monday. In a season such as this they would spend much more time in their car than racing on the track.

On the Wednesday they had another long drive to Derby to take part in the National 25-mile Track Championship, which was run in atrocious conditions with heavy downpours and thunder. Dennis conquered the conditions (working on the land during hard Fenland winters would have toughened him up!) and won another Championship Brassard from Sibbit and Harry Wyld (Derby Police). Being a glutton for punishment he also went on to win the half-mile scratch race.

Next Saturday the Dunlop Sports Meeting at Birmingham was another event plagued by bad weather and the event was postponed until the following Monday evening, when the spectators were allowed in free of charge. The final of the National 5-mile grass championship saw another win for Dennis after he countered an attack by his arch rival Jack Sibbit and powered ahead to open a gap he held to the finish.

A week later the brothers were down in Hampshire at the Poole Wheelers Annual Sports. Some 5,000 spectators watched Dennis beat the local star W. Harvell (Poole Wheelers) with some ease in a series of match races.

More importantly, perhaps, it was here that the brothers met Claud Butler, who agreed to provide them with their machinery and no doubt 'expenses' as well. This could well have amounted to four complete track machines between them. It is probably no coincidence that the following week's edition of *Cycling* carried a half-page advert listing the track events won on Claud Butler machines, many of which were down to Dennis and his brother.

Given the NCU's paranoia over amateur status, cloak and dagger advertising of the bicycles ridden by the top amateurs was the order of the day in Britain during the 1930s. Maurice Selbach had supplied the machine on which Teddy Richter won the 1932 world amateur sprint championship and was involved in supplying machines to the Wyld brothers of Derby, with the eponymous 'Golden Wyld' colour being a much vaunted Selbach frame finish. Equally, Claud Butler was a shrewd publicist for his own machines, surreptitiously advertising that he supplied both solos and tandems to the Horns, the Chambers brothers and also to World Champion and 1936 Olympic Gold medalist Toni Merkens. It was to be the basis of Claud Butler's lasting fame as a builder of quality lightweight bicycles.

'D. S. Horn's Finishing Touch' was the headline for the report on the 21st Meeting of Champions held at Herne Hill on 9 September. Dennis convincingly won the Invitation Scratch Race finals from Londoner, A G Sier, and Austrian, F Dusika. He also attacked the Quarter-mile Paced Standing Start record held by Sid Cozens and managed to equal the time of 28 seconds. No doubt this extra event was included as a result of Claud Butler's flair for showmanship.

In *Cycling* of 6 October 1933 'The Loiterer', a regular columnist, wrote that he considered Dennis (who had yet again secured the Meredith Memorial Track Trophy, amassing 53 points to Jack Sibbit's 19) to be the equal of any amateur sprinter in the world, except that he lacked the expertise to ride on the steeply banked tracks as used on the Continent. These tracks, as well as needing a different riding technique, also favoured different tactics and the Europeans were used to riding them to full advantage. To a Continental rider our 'banked' tracks, such as Herne Hill, wouldn't be considered banked at all and one often reads in contemporary reports that they swerved wide on them due to their lack of camber. On British tracks riders had to turn into the bends and work to keep the machine on course. On the steeper banked tracks of the Continent the camber carried the rider round with much less effort, enabling him to carry a greater speed through the bend.

Looking at the events as detailed above for 1933 it is obvious that Dennis and Cyril must have spent hundreds of hours travelling between different parts of the country. In later life Cyril was to say that when approached by event organisers they would explain that they were far too busy on the farms and that it would cost them too much in lost earnings to attend the meeting. Eventually the organisers realised that they had to pay expenses plus appearance money to get them to appear. Gates were often measured in the thousands and the brothers would be the biggest attraction on the UK track scene. During the track racing season their businesslike attitude towards promoters, coupled with their winnings, must have secured them a reasonable income, as there would have been precious little time left for any agricultural work. It is safe to assume that they received more than just the bikes from Claud Butler, since they also attended shop openings and Claud's promotional events at cycle shows and the like.

1934

At the start of this year an article in *Cycling* on February 16 insisted that: 'Horn Should go to Leipzig'. The piece went on to say that this year there would be an unfortunate clash of dates between the Empire Games and the World Championships, but argued that Dennis should be picked for Leipzig for the Worlds, rather than Manchester for the Empire, because of his showing at the previous year's Championships. The Leipzig track, it explained, was much steeper than Herne Hill and that even the straights at Leipzig were banked to the same degree as the banking on the bends at Herne Hill. It was hoped that this would suit Dennis with his longer sprint.

This was to be a year when Dennis would compete many times against the great German rider, Toni Merkens. Although great rivals on the track, they were to become very good friends once off it. Toni once wrote an article in *Cycling* saying, 'I would very much like to ride a tandem match against the best men in England with Dennis Horn as my partner.' In later life, Dennis told his son that Toni was his only real friend in the world of track racing and it seems likely that during his many visits to England he occasionally stayed with Dennis.

As a result of the way Dennis trained he was never at his peak at the annual Herne Hill Good Friday Meeting, which this year, attracted a crowd of 9,000. The only training that Dennis had been able to do had been on the roads around his home in the Fens, as there were no all-weather track facilities anywhere in the UK. So when, in 1934, the two came head to head for the first time Toni had the advantage of having trained and raced on the indoor tracks in Europe during the lead up to Herne Hill. This disadvantage for Dennis was to show, and the headline in *Cycling* read, 'Heil! Merkens! – Toni Merkens of Germany Sweeps the Board at the SCCU Good Friday Meeting at Herne Hill.' He had won all three races in a triangular sprint match against Dennis and A. G. Sier (Dennis was second in two of them) and also the 550-yards Scratch race, with Dennis again second.

In the middle of May, however, Dennis was in far better condition, and at the Norfolk and Norwich ABC Sports, he avenged his defeats by Toni Merkens at Easter. He retained the prestigious King's Cup, beating Cyril in the Half-mile Scratch Race by a length, with Merkens third. In addition, there was a top-class field in the 3-mile event: virtually all the top national sprinters were in Norwich that day, having hoped to get their hands on the King's Cup! Dennis won the 3-mile race by a length from Merkens.

It was back to London on 2 June for the Grand Prix of London meeting at Herne Hill. Dennis won the 5-mile Point-to-Point, but in the Grand Prix of London it was Toni Merkens who came out on top, with Dennis second, and Frenchman Ulrich third. After the meet Merkens and Dennis travelled together to Copenhagen for the next International Grand Prix to be held in the city. The result was the same: Toni first; Dennis second.

Dennis did not, however, enter the Grand Prix de Paris, and turned down an invitation to ride the Amsterdam Grand Prix, much to the regret of *Cycling*. 'Our star sprinter,' they maintained, 'could do with this stiff competition from the Continental riders and the experience of the steeper smoother tracks if he is ever to compete on the international scene with some success.'

The 25-mile National Track Championship was held at the Derby Municipal Track on 30 June. Dennis won this Championship for the third time in succession and the fourth time overall. The Derby track comprises a cement bowl with shallow banking, nothing like a European velodrome. Dennis rode a controlled race, keeping near the front, not bothering too much with the intermediate lap sprints but, on the last lap, making a jump from the back straight which no-one apart from Jack Sibbit could match, but even he finished a full length behind, .

Dennis could not have done much farming in July: on the 7th he was down in Bristol for the city's Douglas Sports event in the city, where he won the 5-mile Scratch Race and came second in the 1-mile Scratch. That same weekend he somehow managed to take part in the Glasgow Corporation Transport Sports – many hundreds of miles away from both Bristol and home. He won the 1,000-yard Scratch Race, the Half-mile Handicap, off scratch, and came second in the 2-mile event. A couple of days later he was back again at Herne Hill for the Polytechnic CC Meeting, where he won the 1,000-metre Invitation Scratch Race. Starting his sprint in the back straight, he held off all the others to win by three lengths.

TONI MERKENS
The youthful German Champion.   " Full of pep."

Cartoon of Toni Merkens, from the Programme of the
Good Friday meeting at Herne Hill, 1935

The following Saturday he was at Fallowfield where, according to *Cycling*'s report, 'Toni Merkens, the German amateur, who appears to be almost invincible, won everything but the Vi-tonica Cup at the Manchester Wheelers' meet. He is now the Sprint Champion of England, having beaten Dennis Horn by a half-length. He also won the new Muratti Cup'*. In the Vi-tonica Cup Dennis was first over the line, but then disqualified for allegedly having ridden wide and taken Sibbit with him. There was to be an enquiry into this incident at the beginning of 1935.

On the Monday evening both Merkens and Dennis were at Herne Hill for the Norwood Paragon Meeting and Dennis was matched against the German and the Austrian, F Dusika, in a three-match race competition. The first race, a one-lap sprint, was won by Dennis; the second event was slightly longer at 1½ laps and Merkens got his revenge here. It was all down to the final race of the series to decide who was to be the winner. Once again, over the one lap, Dennis came out on top. Dusika was third in all the races. 'This is the first time this year that Horn has beaten Merkens, except on the cinders at Norwich,' remarked *Cycling*.

Next Saturday it was Rugby, the venue for the National 5-mile Grass-track Championship, which Dennis won in style, and the same weekend saw him winning the Half-mile Scratch Race at the Buckinghamshire Constabulary Sports.

At this stage of the season Dennis led the Meredith Memorial Trophy with 39 points to Toni Merkens' 18 points. It is amazing that a German-based rider was able to amass enough points to be runner-up in the competition at this time of the year.

When the Empire Games selections were announced, as expected, they did not include Dennis (who was to ride the World Championships). Dennis was announced as the only English rider to travel to the World Championships, which would be held on the same dates as the Empire Games. 'The Loiterer' commented in *Cycling* that Dennis Horn had a chance, which he would not have given him earlier in the season. Even when his form was discouraging he persevered, knowing that the speed was in him somewhere. He had reached a point where he was beating everybody except Toni Merkens.

Meanwhile in Germany, at Halle near Leipzig, Toni Merkens was winning the German National Amateur Sprint Championship and the 25-kilometre Championship of Germany.

---

* A new Muratti Cup because he had won the previous cup outright.

But at the World Championships things did not turn out as expected: Dennis was eliminated in the 1/8 finals, beaten by Van der Linden of Holland, and Merkens was beaten in the semis. The World Champion final was raced between Van Vliet and the Italian Benedetto Pola, who was the eventual winner.

Meanwhile, back home in the Empire Games, Australia, Canada and England each won a title, Ernie Higgins taking the 1,000-yard title for England.

The following Wednesday Dennis returned to his second home at Herne Hill and was once again 'King of the Castle', winning every race and heat in which he rode. He beat the Empire Games champion easily. Five Dominion riders from the Empire Games were entered for the 550-yards Scratch won by Dennis with Higgins second; in the 50-lap Madison Dennis paired up with Percy Wyld of Derby and they controlled the whole race, winning easily by 7 points. In the 5-lap Italian Pursuit Race between a Dominions Team and the English team Dennis took over on the last lap and turned a deficit of several yards into a narrow victory for England. Comparing the results from this meeting with the previous week's World Championship results does show the difference in the standard of racing in Britain, compared to that on the Continent, which explains why *Cycling* had been so keen for Dennis to get some races in Paris and Amsterdam earlier in the year.

'The Loiterer', writing about the World Championships in *Cycling,* said: 'All sportsmen will applaud Dennis Horn for taking the greater risk of going to Leipzig rather than the Empire Games, where he would surely have been the Champion. One only has to visualise Horn dropping out of the sport to understand how severe is our shortage of class sprinting.'

None of this would have been lost on Claud Butler, whose advertisement for the Lightweight Cycle Exhibition in the Royal Horticultural Hall promised that 'D. S. Horn will be there to show you the latest improvements on Claud Butler machines.'

Nor was it lost on Mr C. W. Wilmott who, at the Norwich ABC Annual Dinner in November, proposing the health of the club, made special reference to their crack path man, Dennis Horn. He had won the Meredith Memorial Trophy for the fourth successive year.

Dennis Horn, Britain's most successful track rider throughout the 1930s, with his Claud Butler track bike.

DSH postcard.

D. S. HORN
ENGLISH CHAMPION 1930-1931-1932-1933-1934
WINNER OF LEON MEREDITH 1931-1932-1933-1934

39

Winning the 5-mile scratch race by some distance, Herne Hill, 1932.

Herne Hill 1932, End of Season 'Meeting of Champions' International Race:
Dennis Horn, Jack Sibbet, Toni Merkens, Albert Richter.

Winter training. Racing at Lingay Fen, 1933. Cyril leading, Dennis on the left.

Herne Hill: the Jack Sibbet/Dennis Horn tandem pairing wins again.

41

Dennis has time to check who came second on the cinders.

Back home on the farm, holding the King's Cup, won at the Norwich ABC event in the half-mile scratch race. Early in his career Dennis coveted the 'dressing gowns' worn by the stars!

Great rivals; great friends. Dennis and Toni Merkens.

Merkens always wanted to ride
tandem with Dennis.

A greetings card dated
1934, the year before he
became the Amateur World
Champion.

Presentation of the Muratti and Vi Tonica Gold Cups at Fallowfield.
Dennis won both cups in 1932, 1933 and 1935.

Whitsun Meeting at March GER sportsground. Start of the scratch race with
Dennis on extreme right.

A studio photograph of Dennis with some of his trophies. Displayed on the wall are four Championship Brassards plus the one worn on his arm. He won this fifth brassard in 1932.

Dennis receiving a special award from the NCU to commemorate his sprint victory over reigning champion Bernedetto Pola at the World Championship in Brussels, 1935. He lost in the quarter finals to Toni Merkens.

Dennis beating Bill Maxfield in the 5-mile race in the Coventry Godiva meeting
at the Butts Stadium, August 1938

Lack of opportunity to ride on steeply banked Continental tracks
always put Dennis at a disadvantage in World Championships

1935

January 1935 started off with a bang for Dennis. Claud Butler announced the opening of 'another new Claud Butler Depot in Harringay' with Dennis present. He was also at the Scottish Show in Glasgow helping to promote a special display of Claud Butler lightweights.

In *Cycling*'s 23 January issue, Claud Butler listed in great detail the results of 48 track meetings in the UK, most of which had been won by Dennis, with some by Cyril, although they could not give the names of the winning riders without contravening their amateur status. It also listed five international and national events and the fact that the Meredith Trophy had been won only by Claud Butler machines during its four years – these were, of course, all wins by Dennis, who was the only rider to hold this trophy.

It was noticeable that around 1933/34 the style of Claud Butler frames had changed from the old-fashioned laid back angles with a long fork rake, to one which would not have looked out of place some fifty years later. The head and seat tube angles were more upright, probably 74/72 degrees and the round fork blades had a much shorter rake. These now matched the frames used for track racing on the Continent and were more suitable for the faster, well-banked tracks on which many of the overseas events were held. Claud Butler's advertisement stated that the 'DSH Path' model had the new upright angles. Dennis of course used these to great advantage in the grass-track events predominant in the UK.

Not quite so pleasant was the need to appear before the Manchester Racing Board's inquiry into the events at Fallowfield where, six-months earlier, Dennis had been disqualified in the Vi-tonica Cup for alleged boring. Dennis was legally represented at the inquiry and Ernie Higgins was called as a witness. The case was dismissed and the matter closed – the results were, however, allowed to stand, i.e. Dennis was deprived of his win. When approached for his view, the national secretary of the NCU, the country's governing body, said that he had not been told of the inquiry!

Whilst Dennis was doubtless out training alone on the cold, wet Fen roads in March, Toni Merkens scored a double by winning the Amateur Sprint Race and the Madison at the Berlin indoor velodrome. Although Dennis often said that he never mixed racing on the road with his track racing, it seems the case that every year, just before the Good Friday Meet at Herne Hill he rode in a local 25-mile time trial. This year it was to be at the Boston Wheelers' first open 25-mile TT. Riding under Norwich ABC colours, he finished in fifth place with a 1h 8m 3s.

The 1935 Herne Hill Good Friday International Meeting was held on 19 April in front of a crowd estimated at between ten and twelve thousand spectators. As we have seen, Dennis traditionally started the season slowly and this year was no different. Despite the basic fitness a winter spent working on the land would have given him, plus his accumulated track craft, he lacked an edge of speed against the international riders who may well have been riding indoor events against each other during the winter and racing the early spring events held on the continent. The Continentals would also, no doubt, have spent a great deal of time getting a good base of road training miles in.

At this meeting Dennis was to meet an in-form Toni Merkens, as well as a very fit and fast Ernie Higgins in the International Omnium, and had to be content with third place. Then, in the Five-mile point-to-point, he punctured. All in all he could only hope to improve on these results as he did more racing. Yet even a month later, at the Norwood Paragon Meeting at Herne Hill, *Cycling* reported: 'D. S. Horn, England's outstanding sprinter last year, is taking time to find his form. He appears to be as strong as ever, as was indicated by his magnificent win in the 5-mile Scratch Race, but his long sustained sprint is missing and he was beaten by inches in the first heat of the 1,000-metres Sprint by C. B. Helps of the Poly.' The following week, at Birmingham, both Higgins and Helps still had the beating of him.

It wasn't until the beginning of June, in the Grand Prix of London at Herne Hill, that Dennis started to show his best form. He won his way through the qualifying rounds to reach the final against Van Vliet, the Dutchman who had beaten him in the Worlds the previous year and gone on to finish runner-up to the champion, Pola. Dennis comfortably won the first race, was disqualified in the second, and lost the third by a quarter of a wheel. He then won the 5-mile race in spectacular fashion.

The following weekend it was back to his home club, Norwich ABC, and racing on the town's cinder track. Once again Dennis won the Half-mile Scratch Race for the unique King's Cup. He also came out on top in the 3-Mile Scratch, and once again became the NCU Eastern Counties Centre 10-mile Champion.

Then it was back to Herne Hill for the Olympic Trials and English Championships. The English Amateur Sprint Championship was the one major national title which Dennis hadn't yet claimed. Some countries restricted their National Championships to nationals, but in the UK the event was open to all comers. Merkens had won the previous year and he was to do so again, beating Dennis and Higgins in the final.

Then came a hectic week that was typical of Dennis's midsummer programme. On Saturday he and Cyril were at Bristol, where Dennis surprisingly lost his 5-mile NCU National Grass-track Championship to Irishman B. J. Donneley. Then to Glasgow, in front of a massive crowd of 20,000 on the Tuesday. The following day their Rover was heading south to take part in a match race against C. T. King and R. Hicks (both Belle-Vue CC) at the Charlotteville Sports in Guildford, which they won comfortably, with Dennis setting a new lap record – that after driving hundreds of miles through the night.

Dennis' rivalry with Merkens was resumed at Fallowfield on 13 July in front of a crowd of 18,000, and this time he was the hero of the day, winning the 1-lap Invitation Scratch Race for the 120-guinea Vi-tonica Cup for the third time, and thus became the outright winner. No mistakes and no disqualifications this time. Then he won his first share of the replacement Muratti Gold Cup, having won the previous one outright in 1933. He beat Toni Merkins in both races.

At the end of that week *Cycling* announced: 'Merkens Next Wednesday: a host of track "cracks", including Toni Merkens, Dennis Horn, B. J. Donnelly, D. J. Corr, J. W. Hinton, C. C. Bailey and E. H. Chambers will be seen in action at Upwell and Outwell Jubilee Sports Club's meeting on the Sports Field, Upwell next Wednesday afternoon.' To those who don't know the area, this is a bit like a small village football team having the FA Cup-winners down to play on their local pitch. To get riders of this class at what was effectively a village sports meet was no doubt due to the efforts of Dennis and Cyril to get their fellow riders to attend. As it turned out, Toni Merkens didn't compete – it seemed that he was unable to get permission from the German authorities – but Louis Chaillot (France) was a fine last-minute substitute.

It was up a notch from the village sports gala when, on 11 August, Dennis found himself on the wooden Brussels track with its steep bankings, competing in the World Sprint Championships. He won his first round qualifier against Antoine (Belgium) – when both were riding slowly at the top of the banking Dennis 'lost' his view of Antoine when he dropped down the inside to catch Dennis unawares, but the Fenman wound up his 99-inch gear to nullify a 30-yard gap and take the race on the line. In the subsequent eighth-finals he met the Italian, Benedetto Pola, the current World Champion and disposed of him easily, which was a magnificent feat! In the quarter finals he was matched against Merkens, who beat him before going on to win the semifinal and then the final from Van Vliet to take the World Amateur Championship title.

While Dennis was in Brussels Cyril scored a double at the Monmouthshire Constabulary Sports, winning the Half-mile and 5-mile Scratch races from Ernie Chambers and Jack Sibbit. It must have been frustrating for the other riders not to get a win even when Dennis was away. Cyril seemed to pull out something extra when Dennis was not there as his results show.

A week after Brussels the National 25-mile Championship was held at the Derby Municipal Track. Dennis, who had to ride most of the last lap with a flat tyre, still went on to win by three-quarters of a length from Percy Wyld. This was Dennis's fourth successive win in this event, his fifth in six years (the other winner was Cyril) so the Championship was kept in the family for another year. Dennis also went on to win the Half-mile Scratch from Cyril, leaving the other entrants to share the crumbs. The following week they made the long drive north for the Cowal Highland Games, where Dennis added the Scottish 1,000-yard championship to his many English titles.

At the Southern Counties Cycle Union meet held at Herne Hill on 12 September, Toni Merkens finally got his wish to ride in a tandem event with Dennis, the Fenman stoking in the 1,000-metre Tandem Challenge Match. However, the Sibbit/Chambers pair from Manchester Wheelers, much more used to riding the tandem, beat them. It takes some time for two riders to become adept at riding a tandem and Toni and Dennis would have had little chance to practise together. However, they probably enjoyed the experience..

1935 had been a highly successful year for Dennis, and he was presented with a handsome trophy by the NCU as a memento for his victory in Brussels over reigning world champion, Pola, at a luncheon in London at the end of the year.*

At the Olympia Cycle Show in December Dennis, along with Toni Merkens and Ernie Chambers, was present on the Claud Butler stand where the 'DSH Path' racing frame was exhibited. 'DSH' was a not too subtle way around the rule preventing any form of advertising by amateurs.

In the winter of 1935/6 both Dennis and Cyril switched their allegiance from the Norwich ABC to the Polytechnic CC.

---

* A comment on the relationship between riders and the NCU is that Reuters had incorrectly reported that Pola had beaten Dennis. Through the NCU Dennis received an apology from the press agency – it came with a covering letter from the NCU addressed to 'Dear Horn'!

1936

At the beginning of January Claud Butler announced his track machine as the 'World's Championship Model', alluding to Toni Merkens' win in 1935 on a Claud Butler, the 'DSH' machine as it was then known.

This was Olympics year and the NCU had taken the unprecedented step of requesting the use of Herne Hill for training on Sundays. To do this they had to approach the leaseholders of the track, Dulwich College, for permission as the lease forbad its use on Sundays. They had shortlisted three potential riders thus far: Dennis Horn as the holder of the best 1,000 metres time, and Jack Sibbit and Ernie Chambers as the tandem pair. Bill Bailey, the pre-WWI world champion, was appointed coach and the Herne Hill track had been regularly used since the end of the 1935 season. The emphasis was not on speed but maintaining a level of fitness and track craft. 'It has been necessary to say as little as possible about this training so as not to give offence to residents around the track,' the NCU reported.

In *Cycling,* 'The Loiterer' wrote a piece suggesting that Dennis should represent England on a tandem, along with E. W. Higgins, in the forthcoming Olympics. He pointed out that with Dennis also being the best hope for the sprint and the time trial it would seem as if England had a one-man team. Such was the superiority of Dennis on the track that in reality he was the only rider worth considering for any of the sprint events. As we will see, however, all this speculation would come to nought.

There are no reports of Dennis having ridden a 25-mile time trial on the road, as he usually did before the Good Friday Herne Hill meeting. Perhaps this was because he had been part of the NCU training scheme for Olympic hopefuls which had been running at Herne Hill throughout the winter. Or, conceivably, both he and Cyril, who was also a prospect at this stage, were determined to rest over the winter months.

Cycling's headlines for the Good Friday Meet read 'Merkens the Master' and it would be hard to argue with that. In an International Match between Merkens, Van Vliet and Dennis the two overseas riders took first and second places. In the 550-yards invitation sprint Dennis 'packed' when he was well beaten by Cyril, so no luck there either. At the Olympic trials held the next day at Herne Hill, Cyril finished fourth in the 1,000 metres time trial with a time of 1m 19.6s, while Dennis was thirteenth in 1m 21.8s. This may have given some of the other participants heart, but year after year we see this sort of form from both Dennis at the Easter Meet.

On 6 May it was announced that Toni Merkens would not be defending his English title, as the German cycling authorities had ordered that he would compete in the Copenhagen Grand Prix. Catford CC, who were to organise the championship at Herne Hill, were considering not inviting Continental riders to compete, 'in order to leave the race open to Englishmen'. Before deciding, however, they stated they wanted to hear the views of English riders.

Back at Herne Hill in the middle of May for the Norwood Paragon event, Cyril came first in the final of the 1,000-metre Olympic sprint, relegating Dennis to second place. Cyril jumped to the front in the back straight but was overtaken by H. Fletcher, who had Dennis on his wheel. Undaunted, Cyril fought back in the finishing straight to overtake both. In the 5-mile Point-to-Point Dennis was third. A week later, however, Dennis won the one-mile Grass Track National Championship at the Bournville Sports ground in front of a crowd of nearly 5,000 spectators. Over the previous night and the morning of this event it had poured with rain to produce a slippery circuit with very hard going conditions, so it was no surprise that Dennis, in his Polytechnic colours, was able to use his strength and bike-handling skills to beat R. Hicks (Belle Vue) and Jack Sibbit (Manchester Wheelers) in the final.

The real surprise came a week later, on the Norwich cinder track, where Arie Van Vliet beat Dennis by three lengths to win the King's Cup. The Dutchman, who had finished second in the previous two world's amateur sprint championships, had beaten Horn on good tracks, but was certainly not expected to be able to reproduce that form on the cinders. This was the first time that a foreigner had won this historic trophy.

The following weekend, at the Southern Counties Herne Hill meeting, Van Vliet showed the same sparkling form. He rode five races and dominated each one. Dennis, it was reported in *Cycling*, 'rode as strongly and skilfully as he has ever done', but he was no match for the Dutchman.

After his slow start to the season, Dennis was now beginning to hit his best form and showing himself capable of defeating any English opposition. Not surprisingly he was listed as favourite for the English Sprint Championship at the Catford CC's Grand Jubilee Meeting at Herne Hill. On the day, however, Dennis's National Sprint Championship jinx hits again. C. B. Helps, also of the Polytechnic CC, came out as Champion after a rather farcical set of sprints where favoured riders, including Dennis and Cyril, were so busy watching each other they were content to let others steal a march on them. Helps won the event by a staggering 40 yards whilst Dennis came second and Higgins third.

After the meeting there was a widespread feeling of despair: none of this could possibly augur well for the forthcoming Olympics. *Cycling* told of rumours that the NCU would send no sprinters to the Olympics. Of course, had the final been decided on the basis of best of three, rather than the 'sudden death' single race, the result may well have been different, but the NCU insisted on keeping to this archaic format even though Great Britain was just about the only nation to do so.

The following week the Continentals were at Herne Hill in force to compete in the Grand Prix of London. Dennis rode his way into the final whereas Helps failed even to qualify and was beaten into sixth place, showing what a farce the previous week's race had been. In the first heat of the final Dennis beat both Van Vliet and Merkens in exactly the same way that Helps had beaten him the week before. However, being the best of three there was room for a change of tactics in the next two races. Dennis came third in the second race and second in the third to finish second overall.

After successful meetings in Manchester (where Dennis won the two main events, the Fort Dunlop Trophy and the Hovis Cup), Derby (where he beat local favourite Percy Wyld) and Glasgow (where he and brother Cyril were the leading sprinters) the brothers were at The Butts Stadium in Coventry for the first major event on the newly cemented track. The general impression was not very favourable, most believing that the 'saucer' shape would have been improved with more banking at the ends, and straights with a lesser gradient. This sort of development on the track scene would do nothing to prepare English riders for the more scientifically designed tracks to be found on the Continent – time and again British designers came up with second-rate tracks.

In July *Cycling*'s correspondent, 'The Loiterer', wrote, 'If Dennis Horn retired England would be completely removed from the sprinting map. It would have a far-reaching effect because it would stop the invitation of foreign amateur sprinters.' To illustrate the point he reported the formidable list of overseas entries for the Muratti Cup where, in front of 10,000 spectators, Dennis had been able to control the field at will for the first nine of the ten miles. At the bell he was in third place, closely following the two continentals who were leading. Then, on the last corner, Dennis was able to sprint around the outside on the shallow banking to snatch victory by a wheel.

That week came the announcement of the teams and riders for the Berlin Olympic Games, and Dennis was not listed. An editorial comment in *Cycling* on 15 July went as follows:

The most notable omission from the list is the name of D. S. Horn. He prefers to stay at home. His sprinting activities in England produce prizes; abroad he wins nothing and loses prestige. His is an honest decision. But had we regarded him as a kilometre time trialist – he put up the fastest time in 1935 – then might he have been a worthy representative and willing to travel abroad to carry the NCU colours.

There is much speculation as to why neither Dennis nor Cyril made it to Berlin. Certainly the pair were both very down-to-earth and headstrong characters, and so perhaps didn't fit in with the 'establishment' team managers and administrators. But there also seems little doubt that pragmatic and financial considerations took sway. Interviewed in 1980, Cyril appeared to confirm *Cycling*'s earlier statement: 'In 1936 I was picked to go to the Olympics … But I couldn't afford to go because I'd got several cups I wanted to win.'

To modern eyes this omission of Dennis by the NCU for the reasons offered is astounding. Britain's best track hope for an Olympic medal was left out of the team ostensibly for no other reason than to enable him to chase prizes at home in order to offset the financial constraints imposed on him by the NCU's shibboleth of strict amateurism. In Berlin Dennis's friend Toni Merkens won the Gold medal. This was a controversial decision as he was found guilty of fouling his opponent in the deciding race, which would normally have resulted in disqualification. After an enquiry, Merkens was fined, but held on to the Gold. However, a closer examination of the 1936 Olympic results overall reveals that many of the other medal winners and high finishers were also riders whom Dennis had frequently raced against and often beaten.

Meanwhile, back in Britain the Horn brothers continued their round of lucrative track wins the length and breadth of the country.

Not to be beaten by Coventry in the badly-designed track stakes, in London the newly completed Paddington Track was declared unfit for high-speed riding. It was announced that the track would have to be rebuilt at the same cost as the original faulty one. The council didn't feel inclined to spend so much money again, so the matter remained in abeyance and the track out of use.

The World Championships were held In Switzerland but the only English rider entered was C. B. Helps – he had his expenses paid for by his club the

Polytechnic CC. He reached the eighth-finals but was beaten by Van Vliet and took no further part in the event.

The 24th Annual Meeting of Champions was organised by the NCU at Herne Hill Track on Saturday 5 September 1936 in front of a crowd of 3,000. Dennis narrowly won The International Sprint Match Race from C. B. Helps. It has to be said the the international representation was somewhat limited, but Dennis was racing with a dislocated bone in his shoulder after two recent falls in provincial events. He was due to have an operation on the shoulder two days later.

In November he was back on the promotion trail on behalf of Claud Butler.

1937

In *Cycling*'s issue for 17 February Dennis wrote an article entitled: 'How I Train'.

As I live in Cambridgeshire, there are no tracks for me to train upon. Indeed, frequently it has been the case that I have raced on Herne Hill track for the first time every year when I have begun the season with the Good Friday meet. As there are no tracks handy I train on the road.

I wear old plusfours, a thick undervest and several sweaters. Twenty miles of easy riding interrupted with some short sharp bursts of speed three or four evenings a week is my training now (February). Owing to the comparative nearness of Easter I have already begun fairly serious training. I need a lot, for I rest completely during the winter and seldom ride a bicycle for weeks.

I never worry early in the season; I never try to get too fit in too short a time. The season is hard and exacting and I like to prepare myself slowly for it. The machine I use for training is one of my actual racing mounts; I always find it best to train on the machine used for racing, because, as you know, familiarity with your own machine spells control – an essential factor during those last few inches to the line.

My preference, even in training, is for high gears; I am a pusher more than a pedaller, and whilst I never lose sight of the value of being also able to pedal nimbly, because of my style I begin right early in the season to develop my muscles. My gears vary according to my plan for the evening, but I usually use an 81-inch gear or one of 78 inches. I use tubulars of course.

When I come in after a series of bursts on the road I have a good rub-down, sometimes a bath and invariably a massage. My brother Cyril and I sometimes massage each other, and sometimes we have the services of an expert masseur. Cyril, of course, goes out training with me, and when I can come off his wheel and drop him quickly, I know I must be getting very fit.

Be regular in your habits; I awake at 7.30 each morning, work hard, eat three meals a day – plenty of eggs, vegetables and fruit. Avoid alcohol and nicotine. Keep your stomach clean; plenty of fruit should be your medicine for sluggishness. Don't overload your stomach – I rarely eat supper, and never train in the morning for fear of straining my stomach.

Above all, be cheerful. Cheeriness means confidence, and confidence in sprinting is absolutely essential.

A couple of months later *Cycling* published an article by their staff writer 'K M D'entitled 'Riding Style'. Of Dennis he said:

Riders get acustomed to a position even though it is a wrong one – and will not bother to experiment... Dennis Horn has realised the importance of this experimenting, and he still believes in moving his handlebars and saddle about from time to time... Horn is no stylist, and he makes no effort to cultivate style. He realises that he has remarkable energy and great power in his muscular legs and arms, and he is content to let these play their part in winning races without bothering any more to try to fit his long, ungainly body into symmetrical lines of correct positioning. He has tried, of course, because Horn is one of those riders who has a great knowledge of track skill and also a great willingness to listen to advice from others; but in his case the cultivation of style has stopped because it had a damaging effect upon his speed. 'Ah', rejoins my persistent friend, 'but how really great would Horn be if he were a polished rider; for look what he can do in a ragged manner?'

There was often criticism of Dennis's style, even in the letters page of *Cycling*. It has to be remembered that Dennis started cycling as a grass-track rider and never spent much time riding on the road. Many time trialists spent much time and effort perfecting the art of 'ankling' and 'twiddling' a low gear. As they spent much of their time riding at an even speed on a level road they were able to do this and probably benefited from it. When these riders took to the track it was often as pursuiters where the same smooth style would be an advantage, as opposed to the explosive style needed by a sprinter.

Another year, another Southern Counties CU Good Friday Meet at Herne Hill for both Dennis and Cyril, and this year they both had some useful speed in spite of their lack of track training. Not that they would have been at a disadvantage, because all the amateur competitors were from the UK. Merkens and Van Vliet had turned professional and although new to the paid ranks had gone straight to the top. The 550-yards Invitation Race had a good entry of 16 riders nonetheless, which meant heats, *repechage* and semi-finals before the final, in which Cyril managed to hold off Dennis for a Horn family one-two.

This was Coronation year and throughout the summer there were a large number of grass-track meetings in conjunction with village sports and festivals and Coronation events. For Dennis this was a particularly successful year on the grass. The Horn brothers' Rover was rarely off the road as they travelled the length and breadth of the country. By season's end he had secured 13 wins and four seconds.

On hard tracks, however, he was less dominant, on several occasions losing races he might normally have expected to win. At Whitsun on The Butts track in Coventry, for example, he won the 5-mile Scratch race but had to settle for second place to M. Schoefield of the home club in the Half-mile event.

At Herne Hill he was more successful: he won two of his three sprints in an International Match Race between France and England, thereby helping England to win. Two weeks later the Polytechnic CC staged the Grand Prix of London, where Dennis prevailed in all three final rounds of the GP to win from C. B. Helps by nine points to five. His win was lauded in the editorial comments of *Cycling*, and they began writing up his chances of winning the forthcoming World Championships.

On Saturday 10 July it was the time for the Manchester Wheelers' Golden Jubilee Race Meet at Fallowfield track. It was a cold and dreary day but 12,000 spectators turned out to watch the proceedings. The most successful of the many visiting riders was Hendrik Ooms of the Netherlands who was unbeaten in five races. Dennis would have been strongly motivated for the

Muratti Cup – he had already claimed two 'shares' over the previous two years, but this time he did not make the placings. He could also only make second in the final for the Vi-tonica Cup and finished second in the 1,000-metre Invitation Sprint.

The brothers' own club, the Polytechnic CC, promoted an event at Herne Hill the following Wednesday evening, but again they were denied first place, this time by C. B. Helps, who beat Cyril in the 1,000-Metre Scratch and Dennis in the 5-Mile Polytechnic Championship.

The following Saturday was the big one – the British Sprint Championship at Herne Hill. Both Dennis and Cyril won their way to the final, along with E. Gorton. The result? There was no result! Cyril was first over the line by a full half-lap, followed by Dennis after Gorton had fallen, but the judges refused to place them.

They insisted that if one rider made a sprint then the second rider had to chase. Cyril had made such a break (not once, but twice, because this was actually a re-run after Gorton had punctured in the first race when Cyril was well ahead). For a short while Gorton gave chase with Dennis on his wheel. Then he slowed down, rode to the top of the banking and came to a stop. Catching his pedal on the track, he then fell off. At this point, Dennis was in pursuit of his brother who was way ahead. In falling Gorton punctured again but the judges affirmed that this was after he'd fallen off. The suspicion, of course, was of collusion between the brothers, so the judges announced no result and that the matter would be investigated.

The NCU again showing that they were well capable of turning anything into a farce. *Cycling* was of the opinion that it would be impossible to prove collusion and that the results should have been confirmed. They also went on to point out that it was the NCU who insisted on three-man finals although, all over the Continent, such events were decided by finals with two riders and being the best of three races. Gorton, the third man in the Horn sandwich, also said that this would never have happened if the event had a two-man final. The NCU sulkily went on to announce, even before the results of the enquiry were made public, that none of the three finalist would be selected for the forthcoming World Championships. Instead they chose C. B. Helps and R. Hicks. *Cycling*'s view was that the NCU had done this as the result of the sequence of events at the British Championship.

The Horns were in a friendlier environment the following week at their local Upwell and Outwell Annual Sports. A three-event match race was organised between Dennis, S. Rose and Jack Sibbit. Dennis won all three events, the One-lap Sprint, One-lap time trial and the Two-lap Sprint. He also won the Half-mile Scratch and the 5-mile event.

Finally the NCU came to a decision about the farcical events at the British Sprint Championships. Cyril, who had sprinted to the finish in both races, was declared winner. Dennis was suspended until 31 December for failing to defend his chances in the British Championships, and for acting in a manner likely to bring discredit upon the sport. Gorton, the third rider, was cautioned. *Cycling* wondered if Dennis would decide never to ride again in view of the severity of the verdict.

It followed this up a week later with an article headed 'The Sprint Race Sensation'. Dennis was reported as saying, 'I feel that it is rather unfair that I should have been the only one penalised, but I shall accept the decision like any sportsman would and shall abide by it. I shall not appeal.' Cyril explained that he and Dennis had trained hard for three weeks leading to the Championships and that he was sprinting faster than Dennis. He pointed out that he had reached the finals by beating top riders along the way. He felt that the result was very hard on Dennis and if it had been him, he would have appealed. Gorton, the third man in the race was upset in that all he had to show for his ride in the Championship final was a letter. He was considering retiring from the sport.

In the correspondence columns one writer observed that 'the severe penalty passed on Dennis Horn for his riding in the Championship will, no doubt, give many of his admirers cause for sympathetic reflection.'

It was also announced that 'Dennis Horn is to Appeal'. Dennis after seeking legal advice decided to appeal. It seems as if the NCU were getting into this suspension lark as, in the next few weeks, Jack Sibbit and C. B. Helps were also sent into exile.

One irony in all this was that the suspended Dennis had already accrued enough points to win the Meredith Memorial Trophy for yet another year!

1938

At the Herne Hill annual Good Friday Meet in mid April, Cyril, as National Champion, was invited to a match race against Jef Van der Vyver of Holland, Bruno Loatti of Italy and Bill Maxfield. He managed a third and two fourths to finish fourth in the match. Dennis (presumably now forgiven) was invited to compete in the Invitation Sprint Match. He fought his way to the final where he finished second to Van der Vyver, who was on stunning form this day. The two of them posted the equal fastest last 220-yard time.

At the end of the month Dennis might have appeared at the London 6-day race, but for the fact that the NCU declined the generous offer from the organisers to put on a supporting race for amateurs (as is done at virtually all 6-days even to this day). In spite of our sprinters desperately needing practice on the steeper wooden tracks, the NCU must have thought the riders could be tainted for life if they shared the same stadium with the pros.

Over the next few weeks Dennis was victim of some peculiar judgements of a different sort. In the scratch race at the Birmingham Post Office Sports he was placed second to C. T. King, although photographs clearly showed that he'd crossed the line first.

The same thing happened to him in the Polytechnic CC Jubilee Meeting at Herne Hill. In the 5-Mile Scratch Race F. J. Willett had got a quarter-lap lead a short distance from the finish, but was being rapidly closed down by Dennis and two Belle Vue CC riders, King and Thompson, who all swept by just before the finish. On the line photographs (in *Cycling*) show that Dennis was the clear winner by almost half a wheel. The judges, however, pronounced King first, Dennis second and Thompson third!

There could be no argument three days later at The Butts stadium in Coventry, where Dennis secured the Hercules Trophy outright by winning the Half-mile Scratch.

One of the big events of the season was to be the Dunlop Jubilee Meeting at Herne Hill on the following Saturday. Dunlop were well known for producing the tubular tyres used by many track riders, so an event such as this would be good publicity for them and they had secured several of the top European professional sprinters for the day's racing. Jef Scherens won the professional match race against Arie Van Vliet, Teddy Richter and Louis Gerardin. In the final of the 500-metre Scratch Race for the Grand Prix of London, Hendrik Ooms of Holland came first, relegating Dennis to second place.

At the Dunlop Jubilee Meeting Dennis was interviewed by 'Sprinter', a reporter from *Cycling*, and the following week the magazine carried a full-page piece entitled 'D. S. Horn's Plans' with a subtitle: '"I am going to try to win the world's championship,' says Britain's strongest track rider in an exclusive interview with "Sprinter", who reveals Dennis Horn's plans for his last season of track racing.'

'Sprinter' had heard rumours that Dennis intended to retire at the end of this season and Dennis confirmed this, adding that he hoped to win the

British Championship which had eluded him so far. After ten years of racing, he said, he intended to make one final effort, as in the past, 'my private business has prevented me from doing so'. Also he would have a serious crack at the World Championships to be held in Amsterdam at the end of August. But even if he did win the World Championships, he insisted he would retire at the end of this season. As for special training for the Worlds, Dennis replied enigmatically: 'Only training by the sea!'

Interestingly, he also offered the view that W. W. Maxfield was England's best hope for the future. 'Perhaps not this year, but he should be able to beat the best in a year or so.'

Just three days later it was Bill Maxwell who inflicted a rare defeat on Dennis over 25 miles at the National 25-mile Track Championship. Dennis exacted some revenge in the 500-yards Scratch Sprint when he beat the Kentish Wheeler by a length.

At the Fallowfield Track on 9 July, Manchester Wheelers held one of their biggest events yet, with races for both the prestigious Muratti and Vitonica Cups. The Vi-tonica cup was contested over one lap and was won by Bruno Loatti (Italy), with Cyril in second place. Loatti also won the 750-metre International Scratch race, this time from Dennis. The Muratti Cup was raced over 10 miles and there was a breakaway by Gorton (winner) and Ralph Dougherty, which was never caught as they lapped the field. Dennis had already retired. Many people thought that this event would be used as a guide as to which rider should be selected for the forthcoming Worlds, but as it was held in pouring rain it was difficult to draw any conclusion, except possibly that Dennis still hadn't reached the fitness or speed that he normally would have had at this time of the year. Perhaps he was planning to peak for the Worlds at the end of August, and the forthcoming sprint championship might provide a better indication.

The headline in *Cycling* 20 July said it all: 'D. S. Horn English Sprint Champion at Last.' The crowd numbered 500, which must have been a record low for a major meeting at Herne Hill. Having learned from the previous year's debacle the NCU had decided, finally, to hold the final as a two-man event. The resulting cat and mouse techniques were not understood by the announcer, who made several derisive remarks, which simply served to show just how out of touch with the continental racing scene Britain was. Dennis won the first race of the finals against R. Thompson by half a length, and the second by four bike lengths. Dennis was riding a 94-inch gear to Thompson's 90, and was simply able to power away in both races.

Dennis's first race as National Champion was fittingly in his home village sports, the Upwell and Outwell Jubilee Sports, where his career had started. It was held on the following Wednesday and Dennis won the 5-mile and Half-mile Scratch races and came second in the Half-mile short limit Handicap race.

Dennis was named amongst the riders invited by the NCU to compete at the World Championships in Amsterdam at the end of August. As National Champion it would have been hard to leave him out.

'Dennis Horn (Polytechnic CC) Still the Master of English Track Sport' ran the headline in *Cycling* at the beginning of August, after Dennis had convincingly won the 500-yards Scratch Race final at The Butts stadium. He was first again in the 5-mile Scratch Race, ahead of Maxfield and Gorton. 'He gave as convincing a display as I have seen him give this season,' Sprinter reported, 'and his splendid finishing dash in the concluding event, the Five-mile Race, gained a well-merited ovation from the large holiday crowd.'

Although the Worlds were only three weeks away, Dennis and his brother continued with what would have been their normal routine at this time of the year: Abertillery for the Monmouthshire Constabulary Sports where Dennis won the Half-mile Scratch Race; a few days later, the City of Ely Sports, where Cyril won the 1,000-yard Scratch race for the NCU Eastern Centre Championship ahead of Dennis, who then went on to win the Half-mile scratch race; then down to Bristol where Dennis won the 5-mile Scratch Race. Finally it was off to Amsterdam.

At the World Championships Dennis was beaten in his first heat by Italo Astolfi, an 18-year old Italian. In his *repêchage* event (a second attempt to qualify by those previously eliminated) he was beaten by Hasselberg. That was it – the end of his participation in that year's championships. Dennis's great strength had always been his ability to hold a high speed sprint longer than anyone else in the UK. On the Continent, because the very different style of tracks produced very different tactics, it was comparatively easy for those used to that type of racing to nullify Dennis's strength, by track-craft and guile.

His disappointment was probably compounded in his first event back at home, the Meeting of Champions at Herne Hill, where Bill Maxfield (who had progressed one round further than Dennis in Amsterdam) showed he was the man of the moment – in England, at least. Dennis was relegated to third place and managed only one win throughout the afternoon.

As a small consolation Dennis had accrued enough points at home to win the Meredith Memorial Trophy for the eighth year since its inception in 1931. He was, in fact, the only rider who'd ever held this trophy.

MEREDITH MEMORIAL TRACK TROPHY

Mrs. MEREDITH has presented to the National Cyclists' Union a Shield, originally known as the Alexander Clark Shield, in memory of her late husband, Leon Meredith, seven times Amateur World's Champion, and winner of numerous National Championships.

The Trophy will be a permanent one and will be held for one year by the rider who gains the most points in certain selected events. Points will be awarded three, two and one, to the riders placed first, second and third in each such event.

The 550 yards Invitation Scratch Race and the 5 mile "Point-to-Point" are two of the events selected for the above Trophy in to-day's programme.

The winner in 1931, 1932 and again in 1933 was D. S. Horn, Norwich A.B.C.

From the Programme of the Good Friday meeting at Herne Hill, 1934

Bending the rules of amateurism? In 1936 Claud Butler announced his track frame as the 'D.S.H. Worlds Championship Model', alluding to Toni Merkens' win in 1935 on a Claud Butler, the 'D.S.H.' machine as it was then known.

6

1939: a year too far

Dennis had stated categorically that he would retire at the end of the 1938 season, but his resolve seemed to have weakened and he decided to ride some events in 1939. He had by now rented a farm at Leverington, near Wisbech. Rather than being a fruit and vegetable agent, he intended to become a farmer. Without doubt it would have been difficult to train to his usual level whilst establishing himself in the new business.

After a certain amount of vacillation Dennis decided to ride at Herne Hill on Good Friday, but he failed to qualify for the final in the 550-yard Invitation Sprint against German, Dutch and Belgian riders. So too did Maxfield, who had spent much of the winter training in Paris. He did, however, win the 5-mile point-to-point, which suggested his time on the indoor track in Paris over the winter had not been wasted.

A month later *Cycling* reported: 'May 11, Herne Hill – Dennis Horn can rarely have ridden this badly.' He finished last in several of the heats and retired in the 5-mile event. The following week, at Bourneville, he (and Cyril) were still struggling to find form in the race for the BSA Gold Vase. Both retired well before the finish. The same happened in the 5-mile event at The Butts Track in Coventry, where Maxfield had a double win. By now Dennis may have wished that he had retired at the end of 1938.

At the Southern Counties CU Meeting at Herne Hill in the middle of June Reg Harris set the track alight, beating Dennis in his heat and going on to win the final. Dennis didn't figure in the results. Nor was he placed in the Glasgow Transport CC event – he had usually been a winner on his excursions to Scotland. Maxfield, by contrast, recorded a win and a second place.

The following day Dennis was at the Manchester City Police A C Sports where he won his heat in the 500-metre Scratch, but finished last in the final to Maxfield. Both Maxfield and Harris had a good day at Fallowfield, and now all the talk was about which one of them would come out on top in the forthcoming National Sprint Championships. There was no mention of Dennis. In the event Dennis didn't defend his National Sprint title at Herne Hill. Maxfield became the new champion, while Reg Harris was eliminated and didn't reach the final.

But for Dennis there was still the Manchester Wheelers' classic event at Fallowfield for the Muratti Gold Cup, in which over the years he had performed so majestically. And, in his last year of competition, what a race it turned out to be.

It had everything – rain, in the best Manchester tradition, great riders: British Sprint Champion Dennis Horn, twice a winner in this series and keen for a third to win his second 'Muratti' Gold Cup outright, and the 1938 hero, 25-miles record holder Ralph Dougherty. After a rather miserable year Dennis was at last in the thick of things again. This was a day when only the hardiest could survive and Dougherty, ably abetted by National 25-miles Champion, George Fleming, set to work to prove it. One by one the stars disappeared, shattered by the cracking pace of Dougherty and Fleming, until only seven remained. Dennis Horn was still there but the persistent hammering by Dougherty and Fleming was sapping away his ebbing energy. At the bell it was still Dougherty forcing the pace. As they swept round the last banking the Midland champion, Morgan shot through to lead – to win? No! Here comes the fighting Fenlander, Dennis Horn, bursting through on the outside – Morgan is beaten – another 'Muratti' is won outright! But, no, another sensation! The mud-plastered, unyielding Dougherty is coming again. Horn looks across at the head-down Dougherty, realising the 'Muratti' is slipping from his muddy grasp. Desperately they battle to the line and with a last superhuman kick Dougherty flings his bike across the line first and the 'Muratti' stays alive for further battles, but not before the greatest battle of all time, World War II, put an end to the 'Muratti' until 1946.
(from *The History of the Manchester Wheelers,* Chapter 5)

As usual, the other big race of the event was for the Vi-tonica Cup, contested over one lap (502 yards). It was won by Reg Harris from Maxfield with Dennis in third place – a result which seemed to typify the changing of the guard. During the best part of a decade Dennis had dominated track racing in the UK. Now it was time to hand over to a new generation of young British track hopefuls.

For the first time since its inception Dennis didn't win the Meredith Memorial Trophy. It was won by Maxfield, and it was Maxfield, D. E. Ricketts and the 19-year-old Reg Harris who left for Milan by train for the forthcoming World Championships. Having arrived in Milan, however, the team was withdrawn and they were brought home without riding (as was the French team) for fear that war might be declared at any moment and the team could be stranded in Europe.

Dennis never again took part in competitive cycling once war was declared; he was expected to work hard on food production as his contribution to the war effort. His personal life took a new turn in that he had met his wife-to-be and leased a farm in order to earn a living off the land.

3.15. Event 5

HALF MILE INVITATION CYCLE SCRATCH

FOR THE

Perpetual Challenge Cup

Presented by HIS MAJESTY KING GEORGE V.

The Cup is a Solid Silver Two-handled Cup on Pedestal, in
the Georgian Style, engraved with the Royal Arms on one
side, and on the reverse is the inscription:—

"**Challenge Cup Presented to
the Norfolk and Norwich and the
Norwich Amateur Bicycle Clubs'
Annual Charity Sports**
BY
**KING GEORGE THE FIFTH,
1911.**"

Holder   -   D. S. HORN.

PREVIOUS HOLDERS:—

1911	Johnson, V. L.	1925	Sibbit, J. E.
1912	Ryan, E. F.	1926	,, ,,
1913	Boor, F.	1927	,, ,,
1914	Johnson, V. L.	1928	Horn, C. W.
1915—1918.	No race	1929	Chambers, E. H.
1919	White, A.	1930	Horn, D. S.
1920	,, ,,	1931	Chambers, E. H.
1921	Ormston, W. A.	1932	,, ,,
1922	White, A.	1933	Horn, D. S.
1923	Sibbit, J. E.	1934	,, ,,
1924	,, ,,	1935	,, ,,

First Prize—Replica of Cup, value £7.

Second Prize—Silver Salver, value £3.

Third Prize—Silver Lighter and Ash Tray, value £1.

First in each Heat and Two Fastest Seconds to compete in Final.

From the Programme of the Norwich ABC Whit-Monday
meeting, 1936. Dennis won the King's Cup five times.

7

Overview

English Rose emblems – steel Claud Butler track bikes – thousands of spectators – championship brassards – riders clad in dressing gowns – real gold and silver trophies – rivals with Nazi swastika emblems – large outdoor hard tracks with shallow bankings – races from a quarter of a mile to 25 miles in length – flat grass tracks at country fairs – handicap events – 'true blue' amateurs – solos and tandems…

To modern eyes, this mix of features that together epitomised the British track cycling scene of the 1930s is a world away from the discretely enclosed 250-metre indoor board tracks of today, on which event-specialist superstars perform before select audiences of *cognoscenti*.

Dennis Horn was one of 1930s British track racing's brightest and best. An all round trackman, he rapidly rose up through the ranks from local rural grass track successes to winning the most prestigious events on the great metropolitan outdoor hard tracks of his day. Furthermore, at a time when British cycle sport held itself aloof from Continental cycling with its professional elite and *en ligne* road racing, Dennis was one of the few British riders to regularly challenge the Europeans on their home velodromes. Over the entire decade he continued to compete at the highest level against an international 'Who's Who' of amateur trackmen. He rode the London Grand Prix several times and he raced in the grand prix events of numerous European cities.

He was also an integral part of successive NCU national teams which competed against visiting teams from Germany, Italy and France, usually in omniums at his 'second home', Herne Hill. In addition, he travelled abroad to represent the UK at UCI world championships: in 1931 in Copenhagen; 1933 in Paris; 1934 in Leipzig; 1935 in Brussels and 1938 in Amsterdam.

However, his major victories and successes all came on home soil. He was the quintessential British prewar 'trackie', and a hugely accomplished all round trackman, a fact demonstrated by his winning the Meredith Memorial Trophy every year from 1931 to 1938.

Was Dennis Horn, the village boy who eventually returned to his family's rural roots when he retired from competitive cycling in 1939, the best 20th century British amateur track cyclist never to win one of the international major titles?

Appendices

The Job of Learning How
by D.S. Horn
(*Cycling* 10 July 1931)

My job of learning how began nearly seven years ago – when I was 15. My brother, Cyril, the new national 25-mile champion, brought Jack Sibbit to our home, and I was permitted to see the famous Manchester Wheeler's English rose, the emblem of a national championship.

I can give no reason why, but I took an instant liking to that emblem and, without fully appreciating the value of its significance, I determined there and then that one day I should wear an English rose upon my breast – like Jack. My brother – six years my senior – laughed good humouredly, when I confided my desire to him. 'Why, you will have to win an English championship before you can wear one of those, old chap,' he smiled. Nevertheless, I made up my mind, and when later I began to race in earnest I was spurred on through those times of disappointment and defeats which must pass the way of all beginners, by the vision, as it were, of an English rose.

A fortnight before my twenty-first birthday there was no prouder cyclist in English than I. My ambition, cherished for six long years, had come true; upon my vest was stitched a plain English rose – like Jack Sibbit's – I had won my first big race and it was the 25-mile championship of England.

And behind my little story of that simple emblem lies a moral, and from the less of that moral is evolved the whole secret of learning how. Just perseverance. Couple with it a flavouring of grit, add a generous helping of determination and a portion of the will to win and you know almost as much as I do. The rest is experience.

There is no set path to success in any walk of life; the road to cycle racing stardom is no less thornier, no less difficult or more easy, as the case may be, than the surface of any jungle track that leads to the pool of success. There is a cyclist of my acquaintance who aspires to be a star sprinter, and who, if merit be judge on strength, training and perseverance alone, should deservedly be possessed of many roses of victory. Something seems to intervene; despite his training and trying, defeat and disappointment have dogged his wheels. It may be continued ill-fortune, wrong tactics or inaccurate judgement, but it is my opinion that he will never be a star sprinter. He is lacking something which is an essential circumstance of a champion's make-up.

Super-speed – a Gift?
I hope I shall not be discouraging the beginner when I suggest that the "something "

is a gift – something born within us. Some men are born writers, others acute business men or engineers or architects or mechanics. So it is with cycling. Sprinting, to my mind, is an aptitude, a special gift. Perfection comes with learning and experience, but the elementary foundation is something elusive. The middle marker who remains as such for years in an excellent example of my meaning; he has experience and knowledge of track sprinting, minus the essential gift of the super-speed which would make him a champion.

I cannot tell you how to become a star sprinter, there is no formula; but I can advise you on the job of learning how to sprint. And then you may discover that the speed and urge of a star are within you. If so, good luck!

An ordinary but enthusiastic cyclist who spends 8½ hours of his day in a factory, behind the counter, or on an office stool has the same possibility of reaching the heights I have attained, providing he is possessed of two essentials: the instinct of speed and the necessary perseverance.

I no circumstance would I advise a cyclist to sprint who has not marked 17 summers upon his chart of life. Enthusiasm at an extremely early age seems far more inflammable and tends to blaze up and end in nothingness far more quickly that the difference of a few years would credit. But it is so, and I would advise no sprinting before the age of 17.

To him who sets a championship as his objective, I would say get a pal for a trainer. Get him to study you, and learning to massage properly; he will be a wonderful asset.

Half the secret of success lies within the construction of your mount . Choose a competent maker, one who is going to take an interest in you, who is prepared to build your machine to fit – preferably one who knows something about tailoring, knows how to use a tape and realizes the necessity for accurate measurements – and who is keen on the game. Adjust your position carefully; ride it a month without alteration. If it then feels necessary, seek a fresh position, but let another month pass before making further adjustments. It may be many months before your body feels comfortable in an attitude for quick and sudden speed, but your patience will be rewarded.

Select small gears to start with, stamina can be built up from twiddling. Be regular in your habits; I awake at 7.30 each morning, work hard, eat three meals a day – plenty of eggs vegetables and fruit – and am in bed shortly after ten at night. Avoid alcohol and nicotine – sprinting and that won't go together. Keep your stomach clean, plenty of fruit should be your medicine for sluggishness. Don't overload your stomach – I rarely eat supper and never train in the morning for fear of straining my stomach. Drink plenty of water. I don't advise a special diet.

Now to the equally important question of training. Be cheerful, never worry, take it as it comes in a happy-go-lucky spirit, but beware less your enthusiasm turns to staleness. Train on the machine you race with, in fact, it is advisable never to use any

other. Familiarity with your steed spells control and a knowledge of its every move-
ment – an essential factor during those last few inches to the line.

Evening training

There is no track in my locality; I train on the road in old plus-fours, a thick undervest and a sweater. Twenty miles of easy riding interrupted with some short, sharp
burst of speed three or four evenings a week is my training. Never be off your machine for more than two days at a stretch; you must keep on getting used to it. To a
sprinter, long-distance touring is, of course, entirely out of question, and so, too, is
road racing, unless it is a '25' at the very beginning of the season, in which it will
serve as useful training.

Walking is a splendid exercise for everyone; it is natural. A gentle stroll – not too
far – should find a niche in every potential sprinter's training programme. Avoid ten-
nis and running, both pastimes reduce sprinting speed. Although in skating exactly
the same muscles are used as in cycling, it is better for the aspirant for stardom to
make sprinting his sole hobby. Study it well; make it a business, but you must be
cheerful. Cheeriness means confidence.

For two months of the 'off season' I rest. Even upon a trained man violent exercise exacts a toll, and for eight weeks I permit my body to recuperate. Two months
before Easter my training activities commence and for the next six months I race
hard.

Mix your distances, try scratch races, but cultivate a preference for handicap
events. Remember that when a scratch man catches you he has been 'slogging' to do
so. Fight him for it, he is probably feeling as 'puffed' as you are.

Before the race

Experience will teach 'on the day' personal requirements, but it is a sound rule
to feed not less than an hour before racing. Between events take care not to catch
cold; rather elementary advice, but it is important that your muscles do not get stiff
through coldness. Far better to keep moving with your jacket and trousers on than to
lie about on the grass in your racing costume. Massage is not vital, but helpful. Cultivate a habit of gently massaging yourself – always towards the heart – whilst waiting
for the bell; it is a profitable way of keeping your mind off the task awaiting you.

The pistol has cracked, the race has begun! Keep steady, watch points, don't
worry, use your head – you know you are fit and can do it – think of winning, that
must be your dominant thought; ride within yourself, remember those last few yards,
conserve your strength and energy; now ready? Jump for it!

Cultivating the Finishing Sprint
by D. S. Horn
(*Cycling* 23 February, 1934)

Stick to Your Training Programme: Regular Habits – Nine Hours Sleep – Building up Strength

How do I train in order to cultivate that finishing spring necessary to win races? First of all let me say that to be a successful track man you must definitely make up your mind on one thing. A man cannot indulge in both track and road racing and expect to excel at both. That is a reasonable expectation. Road racing calls for going all the way (that is, with few exceptions, due to special weather conditions), whereas a track rider has to adopt tactics, use his head and rely on that finishing sprint to get him over the line inches in front of his challenger.

It is said, and rightly so, that a track man rides with his head as well as with his legs. Road racing causes the path man to lose his speed. So let my first advice be this: be sure and make up your mind which it is going to be, road or path, and, when you have decided, stick to your choice.

Jump is all Important

The Editor of *Cycling* has asked me to tell readers how I train, particularly with the view to cultivating the strong finishing sprint which is so essential to a track man – as essential to him as stamina is to the '12' and '24' rider. As practically all of you are aware, the finishing sprint, or jump, wins races, and it is therefore correct to say that the jump is the all-important feature of track racing, and, this being so, should be studied with a view to perfecting it.

A few hints about my training and how I cultivate speed. Every track man's training procedure varies. For my part I cycle five days a week and usually alone. I never ride on club runs, but go out for a brisk short ride at "evens", trying bursts now and then up to distances of 200 yards. In between the bursts I always ride at the consistent and what I think moderate speed of about 20 m.p.h. I do not specifically practise stalling tactics on the track, neither do I indulge in private trials of any sort.

Massage is essential for a track man. Massage and the approved exercises not only improve the muscular and the nervous system, but improve the circulation. No track man's training is complete without periodic attention by an experienced masseur.

The two principal questions that an athlete is asked are: do you smoke and do you drink? Almost without exception the reply is in the negative. Smoking with me is taboo, but there are occasions when I take a little alcoholic refreshment – when I fancy it!

Adhere to Regular Habits

To keep fit one must adhere to regular habits of living, particularly with regard to eating and sleeping. Different opinions are expressed on the amount of sleep that an athlete requires. I have found that nine hours sleep per day satisfies my requirements. Ten o'clock each night sees me in bed and I rise at about 7.30. I take breakfast at 8 o'clock, dinner at noon and tea at 5 p.m. Tea is my last meal of the day. I never take supper.

Do I diet? No! Not for me the special foods – proportions of this and proportions of that. I have never dieted and I am not going to start now. I eat plain wholesome food – and enjoy it.

Now to get back to racing proper. If I am competing in any events on a certain day I train up to the day preceding the eve of the race. That is to say I keep off the bicycle the day prior to the race and forget all about it till the day arrives. I never alter my routine during training.

Stamina and Speed

Before a man can sprint he must build up his physical strength because sprinting calls for staying powers. Not only has a track man got to have that finishing burst but he has to have the strength and power capable of keeping it going to hold off the challenge of his competitors. Keeping that sprint going right to the line calls for plenty of stamina as well as speed. The jump has got to come at the right moment; it must not be started too late or too early. If you go for the line too early your reserve of strength is not sufficient to keep the burst going right to the end. On the other hand, the finishing sprint, if started too late, does not give you the chance to wind it up sufficiently seriously to challenge your competitor.

For a sprinter, position on the bicycle should be carefully studied with a view to one's own particular qualifications and abilities. There are two classes of sprinters: (1) pushers and (2) pedallers. I look upon myself as being in the former class and therefore I sit well forward. It is not advisable for a pedaller to sit too far forward.

Another important point is gearing, and here again there can be no set rule. A pusher would probably prefer a gear higher than a pedaller would choose, and the rider will have to experiment until he finds the gear most suited to him on an average track.

My final word is this: plan your training programme for the season and stick to it.

Dennis Horn's Major Titles & Trophies: 1929–1938

Year   Title/Trophy

1929   Eastern Counties NCU Championship 10-mile (Norwich)

1930   King's Cup ½ mile scratch (Norwich cinder track)
        25 mile NCU National Championship (Derby)

1931   Rudge–Whitworth Cup 5-mile scratch (Herne Hill)
        Dunlop Cup 5-mile scratch (Coventry)
        Norwich ABC 1,000m Club Championship (Norwich)
        Muratti Gold Cup 10-mile (Fallowfield, Manchester)
        Meredith Memorial Track Trophy (season–long competition)

1932   Jordison Bowl ½ mile scratch (Coventry)
        Dunlop Cup 5-mile scratch (Coventry)
        NCU One-mile National Grass Champion (Birmingham)
        NCU National Tandem Champ [Sibbit/Horn] (Herne Hill)
        25-mile NCU National Championship (Derby)
        Norwich ABC 1,000m Club Champion (Norwich)
        Vi–tonica Cup sprint (Fallowfield, Manchester)
        Muratti Gold Cup 10 mile (Fallowfield, Manchester)
        NCU 5-mile National Grass Champion (Batley)
        Meredith Memorial Track Trophy (season–long competition)

1933   Norwich ABC 25-mile road TT (1h 6m 18s)
        King's Cup ½ mile scratch (Norwich)
        Vi–tonica Cup sprint (Fallowfield, Manchester)
        Muratti Gold Cup 10-mile (Fallowfield, Manchester)
        25-mile NCU National Championship (Derby)
        NCU 5-mile National Grass Champion (Birmingham)
        Meredith Memorial Track Trophy (season–long competition)

1934   King's Cup ½ mile scratch (Norwich)
        25-mile NCU National Championship (Derby)
        NCU 5-mile National Grass Champion (Rugby)
        Meredith Memorial Track Trophy (season–long competition)

1935   King's Cup ½ mile scratch (Norwich)
Hercules Trophy 5-mile scratch (Rover CC)
NCU National Tandem Champion [DSH/Higgins] (Herne Hill)
Dunlop Cup 1,000m scratch (Herne Hill)
Vi–tonica Cup sprint (Fallowfield, Manchester)
Muratti Gold Cup 10-mile (Fallowfield, Manchester)
25-mile NCU National Championship (Derby)
Scottish 1,000 yds scratch Champion (Cowal Highland Games)
Meredith Memorial Track Trophy (season–long competition)

1936   NCU 1-mile National Grass Champion (Bournville, Birmingham)
Brooks Bowl 500-metres scratch (Bournville, Birmingham)
NCU Eastern Counties Centre 10-mile Champion (Norwich)
Hercules Cup ½ mile scratch (Coventry)
Fort Dunlop Trophy 5-mile scratch (Fallowfield, Manchester)
Hovis Cup one-lap scratch (Fallowfield, Manchester)
Danish Cup 500-yards scratch (Coventry)
Muratti Gold Cup 10-mile (Fallowfield, Manchester)
Meredith Memorial Track Trophy (season–long competition)

1937   Brooks Bowl 500-yard scratch (Bournville, Birmingham)
London Grand Prix (Herne Hill)
City of Ely Challenge Cup 1-mile scratch
Meredith Memorial Track Trophy (season–long competition)

1938   King's Cup ½ mile scratch (Norwich)
Hercules Trophy ½ mile scratch (Coventry)
NCU National Sprint Champion (Herne Hill)
Meredith Memorial Track Trophy (season–long competition)

Dennis Horn's Track Racing Results: 1928–1939

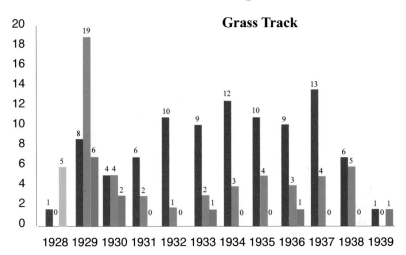

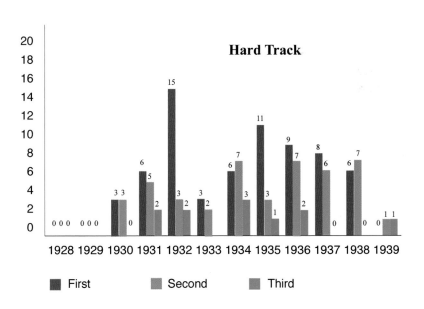

■ First   ■ Second   ■ Third

Dennis Horn's track bike, restored by Colin Bedford and now
part of his extensive collection of vintage bikes.

Claud Butler's advertisement for his 'DSH' track bike

References

CONI (Comitato Olimpico Nazionale Italiano), 1972, *Cycling*, Central Sports School, FIAC, Rome

Fotheringham, W., 2010, *Cyclopedia: It's all about the bike*, Yellow Jersey Press, London

Wadley, J. B.,1975, *Cycling: Leisureguides*, MacMillan, London

Dennis on his wedding day

Peter Underwood was born in Norfolk and started club cycling at about 15 years of age with the King's Lynn CC. He was brought up in the discipline of time-trialling as there was no road racing in the area at the time. However, there were grass track events in many of the nearby towns and villages which first kindled his interest in this branch of the sport, as well as his admiration for those who could ride well on the grass. He continued cycling until a year or so after his National Service, when he moved to Cornwall and became engrossed in sailing.

Some twenty years ago he moved to London and returned to cycling. He now lives in Cambridge and, having given up car ownership, cycles daily.

A re-union with many of his boyhood friends from Kings Lynn CC sparked an interest in the classic bikes he rode in his youth. He and his wife, Patricia, have a collection of classics, are active members of the Veteran Cycle Club, and are joint webmasters of the Classic Lightweights UK website.

* * *

Geoff Waters from Durban, South Africa, also writes on cycle history, with a particular interest in the history of track racing, and contributed background information relating to the administration of the sport at this time.